Easy Soups and SlowCooker Recipes

Cookbook Resources, LLC
Highland Village, Texas

Easy Soups and Slow Cooker Recipes

Printed September 2014

International Standard Book Number: 978-1-59769-202-1

Library of Congress Control Number:

Library of Congress Cataloging-in-Publication Data

Cover and Design by Rasor Advertising, Inc.

Edited, Designed and Published in the United States of America
and Manufactured in China
Cookbook Resources, LLC
541 Doubletree Drive
Highland Village, Texas 75077

Toll free 866-229-2665

www.cookbookresources.com

Bringing Family and Friends to the Table

Delicious and Comforting

Remember when Monday was soup night? Okay, so it was another night, or maybe some of you didn't grow up with soup night, but do you remember sitting down with the family and eating a meal at the kitchen table? Those were good times and had a lot to do with how we grew up and who we are today.

Whether you have soup night, family night, Sunday night suppers or your own special family tradition, we should do everything we can to share these good times. That's why Cookbook Resources created this cookbook and many others like it with easy recipes to help you bring family and friends to the table.

These easy recipes use everyday ingredients that you already have in your pantry or refrigerator. You don't have to make special trips to some gourmet specialty shop. Just go to your shelves or the neighborhood grocery store to find everything you need.

Soup is easy and nutritionally and emotionally good for us. Soup has a way of making us feel better even if we're not sick. When you are in a rush, it's great to come home, open a can of soup, add some frozen vegetables, maybe some leftovers and seasonings, and have a great tasting dish that seems to make the day's stresses go away.

And as soon as you start using the slow cooker, you will realize it's your new best friend. It really does help busy, hassled, over-worked and over-committed people. Prepare ingredients in the morning, go to work or run errands and come back to a hot, home-cooked meal. It's that easy!

We hope you enjoy these recipes for easy, great homemade meals and sharing meals with family and friends. It's one of the real pleasures of life.

Memories are made in the kitchen.

Contents

Chilled Soups

Snacks, Slow Cooker

Vegetables, Soups

Vegetables, Slow Cooker

Continued next page...

Contents

Vegetables, Slow Cooker – continued

Main Dishes: Chicken, Soups

Main Dishes: Chicken, Slow Cooker

Contents

Main Dishes: Beef, Soups

Main Dishes: Beef, Slow Cooker

Main Dishes: Pork, Soups

Contents

Main Dishes: Pork, Slow Cooker

Main Dishes: Seafood, Soups

Main Dishes: Seafood, Slow Cooker

Desserts, Slow Cooker

Conversion to Metric Values

Volume Measurements

Volume measurements are commonly used for liquid ingredients. However, volume measurements can be used for dry and other ingredients as well. This book uses U.S. measurements and it is easy to use metric cups instead of the U.S. cups. The following charts are designed to assist you in converting the U.S. system to metric measurements.

Please note that fluid ounces do not equal avoirdupois ounces (weight). Fluid ounces convert to milliliters and liters. Avoirdupois ounces convert to grams and kilograms.

The basic measurement conversion is:

Liquid: 1 fluid ounce = 29.57 milliliters
Weight: 1 avoirdupois ounce = 28.35 grams

U.S. Cups	Pints/ Quarts	Fluid ounces	Exact milliliters	Metric Cups
¼ cup		2	59.15	60 ml
⅓ cup		2.68	78.86	75 ml
½ cup		4	118.3	125 ml
⅔ cup		5.33	157.7	150 ml
¾ cup		6	177.4	175 ml
1 cup	½ pint	8	236.6	250 ml
2 cups	1 pint	16	473.2	500 ml
4 cups	2 pints/ 1 quart	32	946.4	1 L

U.S. Measuring Spoons	Metric Measuring Spoons
⅛ teaspoon	0.5 ml
¼ teaspoon	1 ml
½ teaspoon	2 ml
¾ teaspoon	4 ml
1 teaspoon	5 ml
1 tablespoon	15 ml

Weight

Avoirdupois Ounces	Exact Grams	Rounded Grams
1 oz	28.35 g	30 g
2 oz	56.7 g	60 g
3 oz	85.05 g	85 g
4 oz	113.4 g	115 g
5 oz	141.75 g	140 g
6 oz	170.1 g	170 g
7 oz	198.45 g	200 g
8 oz	226.8 g	230 g
10 oz	283.5 g	280 g
12 oz	340.2 g	340 g
14 oz	396.9 g	395 g
16 oz (1 pound)	453.6 g	455 g
32 oz (2 pounds)	907.2 g	910 g
48 oz (3 pounds)	1,360.8 g	1.4 kg
35.27 oz (2.205 pounds)	1000 g	1 kg

Length

Inches	Centimeters/millimeters
⅛ inch	3 mm
¼ inch	6 mm
⅜ inch	1 cm
½ inch	1.3 cm
⅝ inch	1.6 cm
¾ inch	1.9 cm
⅞ inch	2.2 cm
1 inch	2.54 cm

A Few Common Ingredients in Grams

Ingredient	1 cup	¾ cup	⅔ cup	½ cup	⅓ cup	¼ cup
Butter	225 g	170 g	150 g	115 g	75 g	55 g
Cheese, cheddar, shredded	115 g	85 g	75 g	55 g	40 g	30 g
Flour, all-purpose	120 g	90 g	80 g	60 g	40 g	30 g
Cheese, parmesan, grated	100 g	75 g	65 g	50 g	35 g	25 g
Meat, cooked, chopped	140 g	105 g	95 g	70 g	45 g	35 g
Sugar, brown (packed)	220 g	165 g	145 g	110 g	75 g	55 g
Sugar, granulated	200 g	150 g	135 g	100 g	65 g	50 g

Slow Cooker Sizes

Slow cookers come in several sizes: 2 to 3-quart (2 - 3 L), 3½ to 5-quart (3½ - 5 L), and 6-quart (6 L) and larger.

The 2 to 3-quart cookers are good for dips, small side dishes, etc. The 3½ to 5-quart sizes are the standard for most recipes. The 6-quart and larger sizes are for large quantities.

Cookers should be filled about one-half to two-thirds of capacity for the best results.

Chilled Soups
and
Slow Cooker Snacks

Fresh Avocado Soup

3 ripe avocados
¼ cup fresh lemon juice
1 (10 ounce) can chicken broth
1 (8 ounce) carton plain yogurt
Chopped chives

■ Peel avocados, remove seeds and cut into pieces. Immediately put avocados, lemon juice, broth and yogurt into blender and process until smooth.

■ Add a little salt and pepper and refrigerate for several hours. Serve in soup bowls with chopped chives on top. Serves 4 to 6.

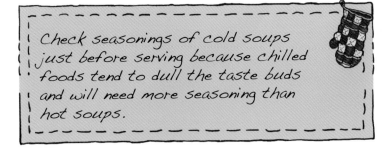

Check seasonings of cold soups just before serving because chilled foods tend to dull the taste buds and will need more seasoning than hot soups.

Artichoke Cream Soup

3 tablespoons butter
2 tablespoons finely minced green onions
1½ tablespoons flour
2 (14 ounce) cans chicken broth
1 (16 ounce) can artichoke bottoms, drained
1 cup half-and-half cream

■ Melt butter in large saucepan and saute green onions. Stir
   in flour and cook for 3 minutes. Slowly add broth, stir
   constantly and cook on medium heat until mixture thickens.

■ Puree artichokes in blender and stir into broth mixture with
   a little salt and pepper. Add half-and-half cream and heat
   just until soup is thoroughly hot.

■ This soup may be served hot or cold. If serving cold, do
   not heat after adding cream. Refrigerate for 2 hours before
   serving. Serves 6.

When leftovers are used in soups,
casseroles, skillet meals, etc. there
are no "leftover" flavors. The dish
has a completely new taste.

Sweet Carrot Soup

1 (16 ounce) package shredded carrots
1 cup orange juice
1 cup apricot nectar
¼ cup lemon juice
⅓ cup honey
⅓ cup sour cream

■ Combine carrots, orange juice, apricot nectar and ½ cup water in large saucepan. Cook on high until almost boiling, reduce heat and simmer for 20 minutes.

■ Add lemon juice, honey and sour cream and stir well. Serve soup at room temperature or chilled. Serves 6.

To keep cold soups chilled for a longer time, put bowls in the refrigerator or freezer before pouring soup and serving.

Chilled Summertime Soup

3 cups chilled, cubed fresh cantaloupe, divided
3 cups chilled, cubed fresh honeydew melon
2 cups chilled, fresh orange juice
2 cups chilled white wine or champagne
¼ cup chilled, fresh lime juice
3 tablespoons honey

- Puree 2 cups cantaloupe in food processor or blender and pour into large bowl. Puree honeydew melon and combine with pureed cantaloupe, orange juice, white wine and lime juice.

- Pour in honey and mix well. Chop remaining cantaloupe and add to bowl. Serve immediately. Serves 8.

TIP: Fresh mint as garnish is always a nice touch.

The earliest archeological evidence for the consumption of soup dates back to 6000 BC. Research indicates that it was made with hippopotamus.

Cold Strawberry Soup

2¼ cups strawberries
⅓ cup sugar
½ cup sour cream
½ cup whipping cream
½ cup light red wine

■ Puree strawberries and sugar in blender. Add sour cream and whipping cream and blend well.

■ Pour into pitcher. Add red wine and 1¼ cups water. Stir and refrigerate before serving. Serves 4 to 6.

Cold soups have been served since the beginning of mankind. They hydrate the body and contain salt and other seasonings, garlic and wine vinegar as examples, that have some medicinal qualities.

Rio Grande Gazpacho

*This spicy, nutritious vegetable soup
made from a puree of raw vegetables is
served cold and is great in the summer.*

1 cucumber, peeled, seeded, quartered
½ onion, quartered
1 teaspoon minced garlic
3¼ cups tomato juice, divided
1 pound tomatoes, peeled, quartered, cored
3 tablespoons red wine vinegar
1 tablespoon olive oil
½ teaspoon ground cumin
2 teaspoons hot sauce

■ Combine cucumber, onion, garlic, and 2 cups tomato juice
in blender.

■ Process until vegetables are coarsely chopped. Add
tomatoes and process again until vegetables are finely
chopped.

■ Pour into medium container with tight lid. Stir in wine
vinegar, olive oil, ½ teaspoon salt, cumin, and hot sauce.

■ Stir in remaining tomato juice, cover and refrigerate for
24 hours. Serve cold. Serves 6.

Creamy Cucumber Soup

2 seedless cucumbers, peeled, coarsely chopped
2 green onions, coarsely chopped
1 tablespoon lemon juice
1 (1 pint) carton half-and-half cream
1 (8 ounce) carton sour cream
1 teaspoon dried dill weed

■ Process cucumbers, onions and lemon juice in blender until mixture is smooth. Transfer pureed mixture to bowl with lid.

■ Gently stir in half-and-half cream, sour cream, dill weed, 1 teaspoon salt and ½ teaspoon pepper.

■ Cover and refrigerate for several hours before serving. Stir mixture well before serving in soup bowls. Serves 6.

An old Yiddish saying affirms what we already know: "Troubles are easier to take with soup than without."

Super Bowl Party Sandwiches

3 pounds boneless, skinless chicken thighs
2 tablespoons Caribbean jerk seasoning
1 (10 ounce) package frozen chopped bell peppers and
    onions, thawed
⅔ cup chicken broth
¼ cup ketchup
⅓ cup packed brown sugar
8 hoagie buns, split

- Rub chicken thighs with jerk seasoning and a little pepper. Place in sprayed slow cooker and add bell peppers and onions.

- Combine broth, ketchup and brown sugar in bowl and pour over chicken. Cover and cook on LOW for 6 to 8 hours.

- Remove chicken from cooker with slotted spoon and shred chicken using 2 forks.

- Return chicken to slow cooker and mix well. Fill buns with chicken mixture. Yields 8 sandwiches.

Nutty Crispy Snacks

3 cups Corn Chex® cereal
3 cups Quaker® oat squares
4 cups Crispix® cereal
2 cups pretzel sticks
1 cup salted peanuts
1 (16 ounce) can cashews
1 teaspoon seasoned salt
1 teaspoon garlic salt
1 teaspoon celery salt
¾ cup (1½ sticks) butter, melted

■ Place cereals, pretzel sticks, peanuts and cashews in sprayed slow cooker and sprinkle with seasoned salt, garlic salt and celery salt. Drizzle mixture with melted butter and gently toss.

■ Cover and cook on LOW for 3 to 4 hours. Uncover last 45 minutes. Yields 2 quarts.

TIP: *You may mix and match other cereals in the same amounts.*

Sweet and Sour Meatball Bites

1 (10 ounce) jar sweet and sour sauce
⅓ cup packed brown sugar
¼ cup soy sauce
1 teaspoon garlic powder
1 (28 ounce) package frozen cooked meatballs, thawed
1 (20 ounce) can pineapple chunks, drained

- Combine all ingredients in sprayed slow cooker and mix well. Cover and cook on LOW for 5 to 6 hours; stir occasionally. Serves 6.

TIP: This can be served as an appetizer or served over seasoned spaghetti.

Pasta has been a very popular food from its beginning, but it was not served on the tables of the rich and famous because it was eaten with the hands. Then a member of the Spanish court of King Ferdinand II invented the fork in the 1400's especially for eating pasta and history was made.

Lazy Daisy Broccoli Dip

¾ cup (1½ sticks) butter
2 cups thinly sliced celery
1 onion, finely chopped
3 tablespoons flour
1 (10 ounce) can cream of chicken soup
1 (10 ounce) box chopped broccoli, thawed
1 (5 ounce) garlic cheese roll, cut in chunks
Wheat crackers or corn chips

■ Melt butter in skillet and saute celery and onion, but do not brown; stir in flour. Pour into sprayed small slow cooker, stir in remaining ingredients and mix well.

■ Cover and cook on LOW for 2 to 3 hours and stir several times. Serve with wheat crackers or corn chips. Serves 6 to 8.

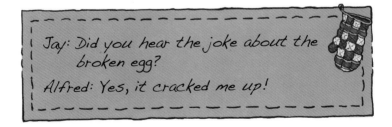

Jay: Did you hear the joke about the broken egg?
Alfred: Yes, it cracked me up!

Spinach-Artichoke Favorite

1 (16 ounce) package frozen chopped spinach, thawed
1 (14 ounce) can quartered artichoke hearts,
**   drained, chopped**
¾ cup mayonnaise
1½ cups shredded mozzarella cheese
1 teaspoon seasoned salt
Baguette chips or crackers

- Squeeze spinach between paper towels to remove excess moisture and place in sprayed slow cooker.

- Stir in artichoke hearts, mayonnaise, cheese, seasoned salt and a little pepper.

- Cover and cook on LOW for 1 hour 30 minutes to 2 hours. Keep on LOW while serving or for as long as 3 to 4 hours. Serve with chips or crackers. Yields 3 cups.

"Do what you can, with what you have, where you are."

Theodore Roosevelt

Unbelievable Crab Dip

2 (6 ounce) cans white crabmeat, drained, flaked
1 (8 ounce) package cream cheese, softened
½ cup (1 stick) butter, sliced
2 tablespoons white cooking wine
Chips or crackers

■ Combine crabmeat, cream cheese, butter and wine in sprayed, small slow cooker.

■ Cover and cook on LOW for 1 hour and gently stir to combine all ingredients. Serve from cooker with chips or crackers. Serves 4 to 6.

Slow cookers usually have two temperature settings: LOW is about 200°F (95°C) and HIGH is about 300°F (150°C). When the heating elements are in the sides, food is cooked on all sides and does not have to be stirred. When the heating element is in the bottom, it is best to stir the food once or twice. Increase cooking time by 15 to 20 minutes each time the lid is removed.

Chicken-Enchilada Dip

2 pounds boneless, skinless chicken thighs, cubed
1 (10 ounce) can enchilada sauce
1 (7 ounce) can diced green chilies, drained
1 small onion, finely chopped
1 large red bell pepper, seeded, finely chopped
2 (8 ounce) packages cream cheese, cubed
1 (16 ounce) package shredded American cheese
Tortilla chips

■ Place chicken, enchilada sauce, green chilies, onion and bell pepper in sprayed slow cooker.

■ Cover and cook on LOW for 4 to 6 hours.

■ Stir in cream cheese and American cheese and cook for additional 30 minutes. Stir several times during cooking. Serve with tortilla chips. Serves 8 to 10.

Honey Wings

16 - 18 chicken wings (about 3 pounds)
2 cups honey
1 cup barbecue sauce
1 teaspoon minced garlic
¼ cup soy sauce
¼ cup canola oil

■ Cut off and discard wing tips and cut each wing at joint to make two sections. Sprinkle wings with a little salt and pepper and place on broiler pan.

■ Broil for about 10 minutes; turn wings and broil for additional 10 minutes. Place wings in sprayed slow cooker.

■ Combine honey, barbecue sauce, garlic, soy sauce and oil in bowl and mix. Pour mixture over wings. Cover and cook on LOW for 2 to 3 hours. Yields 32 to 36 wings.

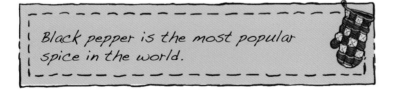

Black pepper is the most popular spice in the world.

Hot Western-Style Sandwiches

3 pounds boneless chuck roast
¼ cup ketchup
2 teaspoons dijon-style mustard
¼ cup packed brown sugar
1 tablespoon Worcestershire sauce
½ teaspoon liquid smoke
French rolls or hamburger buns

- Place roast in sprayed slow cooker.

- Combine ketchup, mustard, brown sugar, Worcestershire, liquid smoke and ½ teaspoon salt and a little pepper in bowl. Pour mixture over roast. Cover and cook on LOW for 8 to 9 hours.

- Remove roast and place on cutting board and shred using 2 forks. Place in warm bowl and add about 1 cup sauce from slow cooker. Spoon shredded roast-sauce mixture onto warmed (or toasted) rolls or buns. Yields 10 to 12 sandwiches.

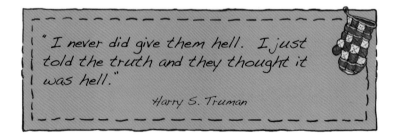

"I never did give them hell. I just told the truth and they thought it was hell."

Harry S. Truman

Hot Open-Face Turkey Sandwiches

1 (2 pound) package turkey breast tenderloins
2 (12 ounce each) jars roasted turkey gravy
1 (28 ounce) package frozen home-style
    mashed potatoes
½ teaspoon poultry seasoning
1 teaspoon Worcestershire sauce
6 slices white or whole wheat bread, toasted
Paprika

■ Place turkey in sprayed slow cooker and sprinkle with a little pepper. Pour gravy over top of turkey. Cover and cook on LOW for 8 to 10 hours.

■ About 10 minutes before serving, prepare potatoes according to package directions. Remove turkey from cooker and cut into thin slices. Stir poultry seasoning and Worcestershire sauce into gravy in cooker.

■ Place 2 slices turkey on each toasted slice of bread; top with ¼ cup mashed potatoes and spoon gravy over potatoes. Sprinkle with paprika. Yields 6 sandwiches.

TIP: You can use 4 cups instant mashed potatoes instead of frozen mashed potatoes.

Buffalo Wing Dip

1 (8 ounce) package cream cheese, softened
1 cup blue cheese dressing
¼ - ½ cup buffalo wing sauce
1½ cups cooked, shredded chicken
¼ - ½ cup minced green onions with tops

■ Place all ingredients in sprayed 3-quart slow cooker and
  cook on LOW for about 30 minutes. Stir well and continue
  cooking until cheese melts. Serves about 10 to 12.

TIP: Add ¼ to ½ cup blue cheese crumbles for more tang.

*This dip is great for any meaty snack or finger food, like
the bacon-wrapped water chestnuts in the photograph
at left.*

Statistical studies find that family
meals play a significant role in
childhood development. Children
who eat with their families four or
more nights per week are healthier,
make better grades, score higher on
aptitude tests and are less likely to have
problems with drugs.

Beer Brat Bites

3 - 6 (12 ounce) bottles favorite beer
Bratwurst
Onions, sliced
1 teaspoon cracked black pepper
Red pepper flakes
Buns
Mustard

- Grill brats over hot fire to get good grill marks on brats. Saute onions in skillet and place in sprayed slow cooker.

- Place brats over onions in slow cooker and pour enough beer over brats and onions to cover. Add cracked black pepper and red pepper flakes to taste.

- Cover and cook on HIGH for several hours until brats are thoroughly hot and soak up some of the flavors. Serve with warm buns, mustard, onions and ice-cold beer.

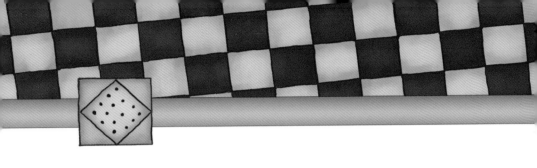

Vegetables

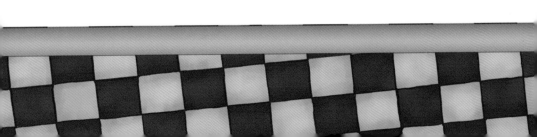

Country Cheddar Cheese

¾ cup (1½ sticks) butter, divided
2 ribs celery, chopped
1 small onion, finely chopped
1 carrot, peeled, shredded
1 (14 ounce) can chicken broth
⅔ cup flour
1 quart milk
1 (8 ounce) package shredded sharp cheddar cheese

■ Melt ¼ cup butter in saucepan and cook celery, onion and carrot until tender; stir often. Stir in broth, bring to boil, reduce heat and cook on low heat for 10 minutes.

■ While vegetables cook, heat remaining ½ cup butter in large saucepan, stir in flour and cook, stirring constantly until bubbly.

■ Remove from heat and gradually add milk. Cook over medium heat, stirring often, until soup thickens, but do not boil.

■ Stir in cheese and heat until cheese melts. Stir in vegetable-broth mixture and heat just until hot. Serves 8.

Potato-Broccoli Soup

3 (14 ounce) cans chicken broth
2 ribs celery, sliced
1 onion, chopped
1 medium baking potato, peeled, chopped
1 (16 ounce) package frozen chopped broccoli
1 (1 pint) carton half-and-half cream
1 (5 ounce) package grated parmesan cheese

- Combine broth, ½ cup water, celery, onion and chopped potato in large, heavy soup pot.

- Bring to boil, reduce heat and simmer for 20 minutes or until vegetables are tender.

- Stir in broccoli and boil, reduce heat and simmer for 15 minutes. Stir in half-and-half cream, ¼ teaspoon pepper and a little salt.

- Heat on medium, stirring constantly until soup is thoroughly hot. Ladle into individual soup bowls and sprinkle with parmesan. Serves 6.

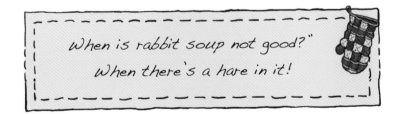

When is rabbit soup not good?"
When there's a hare in it!

Cream of Carrot

1 small onion, chopped
2 tablespoons butter
6 carrots, chopped
2 tablespoons dry white wine
2 (14 ounce) cans chicken broth
1 teaspoon ground nutmeg
1 (8 ounce) carton whipping cream, whipped

■ Saute onion in butter and add carrots, wine, chicken broth, nutmeg, ½ teaspoon pepper and a little salt in large saucepan.

■ Bring to boil, reduce heat and simmer for 30 minutes or until carrots are tender.

■ Pour half of carrot mixture into blender, cover and blend on medium speed until mixture is smooth.

■ Repeat with remaining mixture. Return to saucepan and heat just until hot. Stir in cream. Serves 6.

The first carrots were white, yellow and purple. People in the Netherlands changed the color to orange to match their national color.

Jazzy Cauliflower-Potato Soup

1 cup instant mashed potato flakes
½ cup finely chopped scallions, whites only
1 teaspoon caraway seeds
2 (14 ounce) cans chicken broth
1 (16 ounce) package frozen cauliflower florets
1 (8 ounce) package shredded cheddar
    cheese, divided

- Combine 1½ cups boiling water, dry mashed potatoes, scallions, caraway seeds, 1½ teaspoons salt, 1 teaspoon pepper and chicken broth in soup pot. Bring to boil, reduce heat to medium and simmer for 10 minutes.

- Stir in cauliflower florets and cook for about 10 minutes or until cauliflower is tender. Stir in half cheddar cheese and serve in individual soup bowls with couple tablespoons cheese over top of each serving. Serves 8.

Andy Warhol said he painted soup
cans because he had soup for lunch
every day for 20 years.

Corn Soup Olé

2 (15 ounce) cans whole kernel corn
½ onion, chopped
2 tablespoons butter
2 tablespoons flour
2 (14 ounce) cans chicken broth
1½ cups half-and-half cream
1 (8 ounce) package shredded cheddar cheese
1 (4 ounce) can diced green chilies

■ Saute corn and onion in butter in soup pot. Add flour, ½ teaspoon salt and ¼ teaspoon pepper and cook for 1 minute. Gradually add broth and half-and-half cream while on medium-low heat. Cook and stir until it thickens slightly.

■ Add cheddar cheese and green chilies. Heat but do not boil. Serves 6.

TIP: Garnish with tortilla chips and bacon bits.

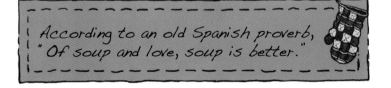

According to an old Spanish proverb, "Of soup and love, soup is better."

Cream of Mushroom

3 (8 ounce) packages fresh mushrooms
1 small onion, finely chopped
¼ cup (½ stick) butter, melted
½ cup flour
2 (14 ounce) cans chicken broth
1 (1 pint) carton half-and-half cream
1 (8 ounce) carton whipping cream
¼ cup dry white wine
1 teaspoon dried tarragon

- Coarsely chop and saute mushrooms and onion in butter in large soup pot. Add flour and stir until smooth.

- Add broth, half-and-half cream, whipping cream, wine, tarragon and about 1 teaspoon salt and stir constantly.

- Bring to boil, reduce heat to medium and cook for 20 minutes or until mixture thickens. Stir often. Serves 6.

A slow cooker works best when filled to between two-thirds and three-fourths of capacity.

Ranchero Black Bean

1 cup dried black beans
3 (14 ounce) cans beef broth
1 large bunch green onions with tops, chopped
3 cloves garlic, minced
½ cup (1 stick) butter
½ cup rice
2 teaspoons cayenne pepper

- Sort beans, rinse and soak in water overnight. Drain beans, transfer to large saucepan and cook for about 2 hours in beef broth.

- Saute onions and garlic in butter in skillet until onions are translucent.

- Transfer onions, garlic, rice, 1 teaspoon salt and cayenne pepper to beans.

- Cook for additional 2 hours or until beans are tender. (Add water if needed.) Serves 6.

TIP: When serving, it is a nice touch to garnish with shredded cheese, sour cream or chopped green onions.

Loaded Baked Potato Soup

5 large baking potatoes
¾ cup (1½ sticks) butter
⅔ cup flour
6 cups milk
1 (8 ounce) package shredded cheddar cheese, divided
1 (3 ounce) package real bacon bits
1 bunch fresh green onions, chopped, divided
1 (8 ounce) carton sour cream

- Cook potatoes in microwave or bake for 1 hour at 400°F (205°C). Cut potatoes in half lengthwise, scoop out flesh and save. Discard potato shells.

- Melt butter in large soup pot over low heat, add flour and stir until smooth. Gradually add milk and cook over medium heat, stirring constantly, until mixture thickens.

- Stir in potatoes, half cheese, bacon bits, 2 tablespoons green onions and a little salt and pepper. Cook until hot, but do not boil.

- Stir in sour cream and cook just until hot. Spoon into soup bowls and sprinkle remaining cheese and green onions over each serving. Serves 6.

Fireside Pumpkin Harvest

1 (8 ounce) package fresh mushrooms, sliced
3 tablespoons butter
¼ cup flour
2 (14 ounce) cans vegetable broth
1 (15 ounce) can cooked pumpkin
1 (1 pint) carton half-and-half cream
2 tablespoons honey
2 tablespoons sugar
1 teaspoon ground nutmeg

■ Saute mushrooms in butter in large saucepan. Add flour, stir well and gradually add broth. Bring to a boil and simmer for 2 minutes or until mixture thickens.

■ Stir in pumpkin, half-and-half cream, honey, sugar and nutmeg. Stir constantly until soup is thoroughly hot. Serves 6.

TIP: If you have some sour cream, a dollop of sour cream on top of the soup is a very nice garnish.

If your soup is not intended as the main course, you can count on one quart to serve six people. As a main dish, plan on two servings per quart.

Homemade Tomato Soup

3 (15 ounce) cans whole tomatoes with liquid
1 (14 ounce) can chicken broth
1 tablespoon sugar
1 tablespoon minced garlic
1 tablespoon balsamic vinegar
¾ cup whipping cream

- Puree tomatoes in batches with blender and pour into large saucepan. Add chicken broth, sugar, garlic, balsamic vinegar and a little salt.

- Bring to a boil, reduce heat and simmer for 15 minutes.

- Pour in whipping cream, stir constantly and heat until soup is thoroughly hot. Serves 4.

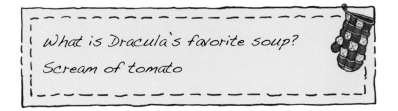

What is Dracula's favorite soup?

Scream of tomato

Fiesta Tortilla Soup con Queso

3 (14 ounce) cans chicken broth
2 (15 ounce) cans stewed tomatoes
4 green onions with tops, chopped
1 (7 ounce) cans diced green chilies
1 clove garlic, minced
8 corn tortillas
2 tablespoons oil
1 (16 ounce) package cubed Mexican Velveeta® cheese

■ Pour chicken broth, tomatoes, onions, green chilies and garlic in large saucepan and heat on medium.

■ Cut tortillas into long, narrow strips. Fry tortilla strips with hot oil in skillet for about 10 seconds or until strips are crisp. Remove from skillet and drain.

■ Heat soup to boiling, reduce heat to low and stir in cheese. Serve in individual bowls and garnish with tortilla strips. Serves 8.

Choice Tomato-Ravioli

1 (15 ounce) can Italian stewed tomatoes
2 (14 ounce) cans chicken broth
1 (12 ounce) package refrigerated cheese ravioli
2 small zucchini, sliced
4 fresh green onions, sliced

■ Combine tomatoes, chicken broth and 1 teaspoon pepper in large saucepan. Bring to boil, reduce heat and simmer for 5 minutes.

■ Add ravioli and zucchini and bring to boil, reduce heat and simmer for 8 to 10 minutes or until ravioli are tender. Sprinkle a few sliced green onions over each individual serving. Serve 6.

The Italian word "zuppa" once described a soup served over a thick piece of bread. Throughout history, people have used bread to thicken soup and add substance to broth. Today the term "zuppa" simply means a thick soup.

Warm-Your-Soul Soup

3 (14 ounce) cans chicken broth
1 (15 ounce) can Italian-stewed tomatoes with liquid
½ cup chopped onion
¾ cup chopped celery
1 carrot, sliced
½ (12 ounce) box fettuccini

- Combine chicken broth, tomatoes, onion, celery and carrot in large soup pot. Bring to a boil and simmer until onion, celery and carrot are almost done.

- Add fettuccini and cook according to package directions. Season with a little salt and pepper. Serves 6.

You can give canned broth a little extra flavor by simmering reserved chicken or meat bones in the broth for 15 minutes. Strain the liquid and use it for your soup.

Quick Vegetarian Chili

2 (15 ounce) cans stewed tomatoes
1 (15 ounce) can kidney beans, rinsed, drained
1 (15 ounce) can pinto beans with liquid
1 onion, chopped
1 green bell pepper, seeded, chopped
1 tablespoon chili powder
1 (12 ounce) package shell macaroni, optional
¼ cup (½ stick) butter, sliced

■ Combine tomatoes, kidney beans, pinto beans, onion, bell pepper, chili powder and 1 cup water in soup pot. Cover and cook on medium heat for 1 hour.

■ Cook macaroni according to package directions, drain and add butter. Stir until butter melts. Add macaroni to chili and mix well. Serves 6.

If you cook pasta before adding it to soup, you can prevent overcooking. Add cooked pasta just before serving. Leftover pasta works well too.

Delicious Broccoli-Cheese Soup

1 (12 ounce) package cubed Velveeta® cheese
1 (16 ounce) package frozen chopped broccoli, thawed
1 (1 ounce) packet white sauce mix
1 (1 ounce) packet dry vegetable soup mix
1 (12 ounce) can evaporated milk
1 (14 ounce) can chicken broth

■ Melt Velveeta® in double boiler before pouring into slow
  cooker. Combine all ingredients plus 2 cups water in large
  sprayed slow cooker and stir well.

■ Cover and cook on LOW for 6 to 7 hours or on HIGH for
  3 hours 30 minutes to 4 hours. Stir 1 hour before serving
  time. Serves 6.

Some of the greatest artists in
history were inspired by soup: Pablo
Picasso painted "La Soupe"; Vincent
van Gogh painted "Bowls and Bottles";
and James McNeill Whistler painted
"Soupe a Trois Sous".

Ultimate Cheddar Cheese Soup

1 onion, finely chopped
1 red bell pepper, seeded, finely chopped
½ cup (1 stick) butter, melted
1 (16 ounce) package shredded extra sharp
    cheddar cheese
1 cup finely grated carrots
1 (14 ounce) can chicken broth
½ teaspoon minced garlic
2 tablespoons cornstarch
1 (1 pint) carton half-and-half cream

■ Combine onion, bell pepper, butter, cheese, carrots, broth, garlic and a little pepper in sprayed slow cooker. Cover and cook on LOW for 5 to 7 hours.

■ Mix cornstarch with about 2 tablespoons half-and-half cream in bowl until mixture is smooth; stir in remaining cream.

■ Stir in cream mixture in slow cooker, cover and cook for additional 15 to 20 minutes or until soup is thoroughly hot. Serves 6.

TIP: Top with a little shredded mozzarella cheese for an
     interesting presentation.

Hearty Broccoli-Potato Soup

3 (14 ounce) cans chicken broth
3 ribs celery, sliced
1 onion, finely chopped
1 medium potato, peeled, chopped
1 (16 ounce) package frozen chopped broccoli, thawed
1 (1 pint) carton half-and-half cream
1 (5 ounce) package grated parmesan cheese

■ Combine broth, celery, onion, potato, broccoli, half-and-half cream and 1 teaspoon salt in sprayed slow cooker. Cover and cook on LOW for 6 to 8 hours.

■ Spoon soup in individual soup bowls and top with a little parmesan cheese. Serves 6.

Soup has its origin as a word from 'sop' or 'sup', meaning the slice of bread on which the broth was poured.

Busy Bean-Barley Bounty

2 (15 ounce) cans pinto beans with liquid
3 (14 ounce) cans chicken broth
½ cup quick-cooking barley
1 (15 ounce) can Italian stewed tomatoes

■ Combine beans, broth, barley, stewed tomatoes and
½ teaspoon pepper in sprayed slow cooker and stir well.

■ Cover and cook on LOW for 4 to 5 hours. Serves 6 to 8.

Before tomatoes were brought to
Europe from the Americas, pasta was
generally eaten with seasoning or cheese.
Tomatoes revolutionized pasta. Italy had
an ideal growing climate for tomatoes.
Tomato sauces were popular with pasta
by the early 1800's.

Screwy Rotini-Veggie Soup

1 (32 ounce) carton chicken broth
1 (12 ounce) can tomato juice
2 carrots, peeled, sliced
3 ribs celery, chopped
1 onion, chopped
1 (15 ounce) can stewed tomatoes
1 teaspoon dried basil
1 (10 ounce) package frozen green peas, thawed
1 (8 ounce) package whole wheat rotini
   (corkscrew) pasta

■ Combine broth, juice, carrots, celery, onion, tomatoes, basil and
a little salt and pepper in sprayed slow cooker. Cover and cook
on LOW for 8 to 9 hours.

■ Increase heat to HIGH and stir in peas and pasta. Cover and
cook for additional 15 to 20 minutes or until pasta is tender.
Serves 8 to 10.

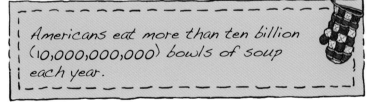

Americans eat more than ten billion (10,000,000,000) bowls of soup each year.

Quick-and-Easy French Onion Soup

¼ cup (½ stick) butter
3 large onions, sliced
3 (14 ounce) cans beef broth
1 teaspoon Worcestershire sauce
½ cup dry white wine
Butter, softened
8 thick slices French bread, toasted
1 cup grated gruyere or parmesan cheese

■ Melt butter in skillet over medium heat. Stir in onions and cook for about 15 minutes or until onions are soft and very light brown.

■ Place onions in sprayed slow cooker and add broth, Worcestershire and wine. Cover and cook on LOW for 4 to 4 hours 30 minutes.

■ Spread light layer of butter on each slice of toasted bread. Ladle soup into 4 individual ovenproof bowls; top with slices of toasted bread and cheese; and place in oven at 400°F (205°C) to melt cheese. Serves 4.

French Onion Soup

5 - 6 sweet onions, thinly sliced
1 clove garlic, minced
2 tablespoons butter
2 (14 ounce) cans beef broth
2 teaspoons Worcestershire sauce
6 (1 inch) slices French bread
6 slices Swiss cheese

■ Cook onions and garlic on low heat (do not brown) in hot butter in large skillet for about 20 minutes and stir several times.

■ Transfer onion mixture to sprayed 4 to 5-quart slow cooker. Add beef broth, Worcestershire sauce and 1 cup water.

■ Cover and cook on LOW for 5 to 8 hours or on HIGH for 2 hours 30 minutes to 3 hours.

■ Before serving soup, toast bread slices and place cheese slice on top. Broil for 3 to 4 minutes or until cheese is light brown and bubbles. Ladle soup into bowls and top with toast. Serves 6.

Cheesy Bacon-Potato Soup

3½ pounds red potatoes, cubed
1 onion, chopped
1 (32 ounce) carton chicken broth
1 pint half-and-half cream
1 (8 ounce) package shredded cheddar cheese
1 (4 ounce) package prepared bacon bits

- Place potatoes and onions in sprayed slow cooker. Combine broth, 1 teaspoon each of salt and pepper; add to slow cooker. Cover and cook on HIGH for 3 to 4 hours.

- Mash mixture and add half-and-half cream. Cover and cook for additional 20 minutes. Top each serving with cheese and bacon bits. Serves 6.

When your family is hungry and the budget is tight, few dishes are as comforting as a hearty soup or stew.

Creamy Tomato Soup

2 (28 ounce) cans diced tomatoes
¼ cup (½ stick) butter, melted
2 tablespoons brown sugar
2 tablespoons tomato paste
2 tablespoons flour
1 (14 ounce) can chicken broth
1 (8 ounce) carton whipping cream

■ Drain tomatoes (reserving liquid) and place in blender; puree tomatoes and pour into sprayed slow cooker. Add reserved liquid, butter, brown sugar, tomato paste and ½ teaspoon salt.

■ Mix flour with about ½ cup broth in bowl until mixture is smooth and stir in remaining broth. Add flour-broth mixture to cooker. Cover and cook on LOW for 6 to 8 hours.

■ Stir in cream, cover and cook for additional 20 minutes or until soup is thoroughly hot. Serves 6.

Summertime Zucchini Soup

1 small onion, very finely chopped
3½ - 4 cups grated zucchini with peels
2 (14 ounce) cans chicken broth
1 teaspoon seasoned salt
1 teaspoon dried dill weed
2 tablespoons butter, melted
1 (8 ounce) carton sour cream

- Combine all ingredients except sour cream with a little pepper in sprayed small slow cooker.

- Cover and cook on LOW for 2 hours. Fold in sour cream, cover and cook for about 10 minutes or just until soup is hot. Serves 4.

The Lone Ranger comes into town on a hot, dry day and gets off his horse. He tells Tonto to get his saddle blanket and wave it up and down while running around the horses to keep them cool. The Lone Ranger goes into the general store for supplies. Soon a big burly man comes into the store and says, "Is that your white horse out there?" "Yes, it is," said the Lone Ranger. The man said, "Did ya know ya left yur injun runnin'?"

Souper Fettuccini

1 (32 ounce) carton chicken broth
2 (15 ounce) cans Italian-stewed tomatoes
1 onion, chopped
2 ribs celery, sliced
1 (8 ounce) box fettuccini

- Combine broth, tomatoes, onion and celery in sprayed slow cooker. Cover and cook on LOW for 4 to 6 hours.

- Cook fettuccini according to package directions, drain and add to cooker. Cover and cook for additional 20 minutes for flavors to blend. Serves 4 to 6.

Tomato-Ravioli Soup

2 (15 ounce) can stewed tomatoes
2 (14 ounce) cans chicken broth
¾ teaspoon Italian seasoning
2 small zucchini, sliced
1 onion, chopped
1 (9 ounce) package refrigerated cheese ravioli

- Combine tomatoes, broth, Italian seasoning, zucchini, onion and ½ cup water in sprayed slow cooker. Cover and cook on LOW for 3 to 4 hours.

- Stir in ravioli, cover and cook for additional 1 hour. Serves 4 to 6.

Handy Corn Chowder

2 medium potatoes, peeled, diced
1 (10 ounce) package frozen chopped bell peppers and
    onions, thawed
1 (15 ounce) can cream-style corn
1 (15 ounce) can whole kernel corn
1 (10 ounce) can cream of celery soup
1 teaspoon seasoned salt
2 tablespoons cornstarch
1 (14 ounce) can chicken broth, divided
1 (8 ounce) carton whipping cream

■ Combine potatoes, bell pepper-onion mixture, cream-style
corn, corn, soup and seasoned salt in sprayed slow cooker.

■ In small bowl, combine cornstarch and about ¼ cup of
the broth and stir until mixture is smooth; stir in remaining
broth and add to slow cooker. Cover and cook on LOW
heat for 6 to 8 hours.

■ Stir in whipping cream; cover and cook additional 15 to
20 minutes or until chowder is thoroughly hot. Serves 6.

Big Bean Mix

2 (15 ounce) cans garbanzo beans, drained
1 (15 ounce) can red kidney beans, drained
1 (15 ounce) can cannellini beans, drained
2 (15 ounce) cans great northern beans, drained
1 teaspoon Italian seasoning
1 (1 ounce) packet onion soup mix
1 teaspoon minced garlic
½ cup beef broth

Combine all ingredients in sprayed slow cooker and stir well.
Cover and cook on LOW for 5 to 6 hours or on HIGH for
2 hours 30 minutes to 3 hours. Serves 6 to 8.

Corn-Bean Mix-up

1 (15 ounce) can pinto beans, drained
1 (15 ounce) can black beans, rinsed, drained
1 (10 ounce) package frozen corn
1 (15 ounce) can tomato sauce
1 (1 ounce) packet chili seasoning
2 (15 ounce) cans Mexican stewed tomatoes with liquid

■ Combine pinto beans, black beans, corn, tomato sauce,
  chili seasoning, tomatoes and 1 cup water in sprayed slow
  cooker; mix well. Cover and cook on LOW for 6 to 7 hours.
  Serves 6.

Creamy Macaroni and Cheese

2 cups macaroni
1 (10 ounce) can cheddar cheese soup
¼ cup butter
2 soup cans milk
2½ cups shredded sharp cheddar or 4-cheese blend
½ cup sour cream

- Cook macaroni on boiling water for 6 minutes and drain well. Combine soup, butter and milk in saucepan over medium heat until mixture blends well. Pour into sprayed 3 to 4-quart slow cooker.

- Whisk in shredded cheese, sour cream and about ½ teaspoon each of salt and pepper. Close lid and cook on LOW for 2½ to 3 hours. Serves 4 to 6.

TIP: *If you like "crispy" cheese on top, pour macaroni and cheese into baking dish. Sprinkle ¼ to ½ cup shredded cheese on top and bake at 400°F (205°C) for about 10 minutes or until cheese browns.*

A couple of drops of hot sauce is a good addition to this wonderful, classic dish. It can add a little zip to life.

Cajun Beans and Rice

1 pound dry black or kidney beans
2 onions, chopped
2 teaspoons minced garlic
1 tablespoon ground cumin
1 (14 ounce) can chicken broth
1 cup instant brown rice

■ Place beans in saucepan, cover with water and soak
   overnight.

■ Combine beans, onion, garlic, cumin, chicken broth,
   2 teaspoons salt and 2 cups water in sprayed 4 to 5-quart
   slow cooker.

■ Cover and cook on LOW for 4 to 6 hours.

■ Stir in instant rice, cover and cook for additional
   20 minutes. Serves 4 to 6.

TIP: *If soaking beans overnight is not an option, place*
       beans in saucepan and add enough water to cover
       by 2 inches. Bring to a boil, reduce heat and simmer for
       10 minutes. Let stand for 1 hour, drain and rinse beans.

Italian-Style Beans and Rice

1 (16 ounce) package frozen chopped bell peppers and
    onions, thawed
2 (15 ounce) cans Italian stewed tomatoes
1 (4 ounce) can diced green chilies
2 (15 ounce) cans great northern beans,
    rinsed, drained
1 teaspoon Italian seasoning
1 (14 ounce) can chicken broth
¼ teaspoon cayenne pepper
2 cups instant rice

■ Combine bell peppers and onions, stewed tomatoes,
green chilies, beans, Italian seasoning, broth and ½ cup
water in sprayed slow cooker. Cover and cook on LOW
for 5 to 7 hours.

■ Stir in cayenne pepper and rice, cover and cook for
30 minutes or until rice is tender. Serves 8.

Dried beans need to be soft before
they are added to the slow cooker
to cook. Be sure to soak beans
overnight or soak for 1 hour and boil for
about 10 minutes.

Crunchy Green Bean Casserole

2 (16 ounce) packages frozen whole green beans, thawed
3 ribs celery, diagonally sliced
1 red bell pepper, julienned
2 (11 ounce) cans sliced water chestnuts, drained
½ cup slivered almonds
1 (10 ounce) can cream of chicken soup
1 (3 ounce) can french-fried onions

- Combine green beans, celery, bell pepper, water chestnuts and almonds in sprayed slow cooker. Heat soup with about ¼ cup water to thin soup just enough so you can pour it over vegetable mixture.

- Cover and cook on LOW for 2 to 4 hours.

- Preheat oven to 400°F (205°C). Place in baking dish, top with fried onions and bake for 5 to 10 minutes. Serves 6 to 8.

Perfect Cinnamon Carrots

2 (16 ounce) packages baby carrots
¾ cup packed brown sugar
¼ cup honey
½ cup orange juice
2 tablespoons butter, melted
¾ teaspoon ground cinnamon

- Place carrots in sprayed slow cooker.

- Combine brown sugar, honey, orange juice, butter and cinnamon in bowl and mix well. Pour over carrots and stir to make sure sugar-cinnamon mixture coats carrots. Cover and cook on LOW for 3 hours 30 minutes to 4 hours and stir twice during cooking time.

- About 20 minutes before serving, use slotted spoon to transfer carrots to serving dish and cover to keep warm.

- Pour liquid from cooker into saucepan; boil for several minutes until liquid reduces by half. Spoon over carrots in serving dish. Serves 6 to 8.

The Onion Solution

2 (10 ounce) bags frozen small whole onions, thawed
2 ribs celery, very thinly sliced
1 green bell pepper, seeded, chopped
¼ cup (½ stick) butter, melted
1 tablespoon red wine vinegar
2 tablespoons brown sugar
½ teaspoon seasoned salt

■ Combine onions, celery, bell pepper, melted butter, vinegar, brown sugar, seasoned salt and pepper in bowl; toss to coat vegetables well. Spoon into sprayed slow cooker.

■ Cover and cook on LOW for 4 hours to 4 hours 30 minutes. Serves 6.

" I am only one, but I am one. I cannot do everything, but I can do something. And because I cannot do everything, I will not refuse to do the something that I can do. What I can do, I should do. And what I should do, by the grace of God, I will do."

Edward Everett Hale

Sweet Potatoes and Pineapple

3 (15 ounce) cans sweet potatoes, drained
½ (20 ounce) can pineapple pie filling
2 tablespoons butter, melted
½ cup packed brown sugar
½ teaspoon ground cinnamon

- Place sweet potatoes, pie filling, melted butter, brown sugar and cinnamon in sprayed slow cooker and lightly stir. Cover and cook on LOW for 2 to 3 hours.

Topping:

1 cup packed light brown sugar
3 tablespoons butter, melted
½ cup flour
1 cup coarsely chopped nuts

- While sweet potato mixture cooks, combine topping ingredients in bowl and spread out on foil-lined baking pan. Preheat oven to 350°F (175°C) and bake for 15 to 20 minutes. When ready to serve, sprinkle topping over sweet potatoes. Serves 6 to 8.

Yummy Bread Stuffing

¾ cup (1½ sticks) butter
2 medium onions, finely chopped
3 ribs celery, sliced
12 cups day-old bread cubes
2 teaspoons dried sage
1 teaspoon poultry seasoning
1 (32 ounce) carton chicken broth
2 eggs, beaten

- Melt butter in skillet and cook onion and celery until they are translucent, about 10 minutes. Place in large bowl and add bread cubes, sage and poultry seasoning.

- Stir in just enough broth to moisten. (You may not use all the broth.) Stir in beaten eggs and spoon into sprayed slow cooker.

- Cover and cook on HIGH for 45 minutes; reduce heat to LOW and cook for 4 to 6 hours. Serves 12.

Most pastas will retain their texture better if cooked separately and either added at the end of the slow cooker's cooking time or simply served with the finished dish.

Garlic-Roasted Potatoes

18 - 20 small, golden or red potatoes with peels
½ cup (1 stick) butter, melted
¼ cup snipped fresh rosemary
2 cloves garlic, minced
1 tablespoon dried parsley

- Combine all ingredients plus ½ teaspoon each of salt and pepper in sprayed slow cooker and mix well.

- Cover and cook on LOW for 7 hours or on HIGH for 3 hours 30 minutes to 4 hours.

- When ready to serve, remove potatoes with slotted spoon to serving dish and cover to keep warm.

- Add about 2 tablespoons water to liquid in cooker and stir until juices blend well. Pour mixture over potatoes. Serves 4 to 6.

TIP: If you want potatoes brown on outside, brown them in skillet with a little oil over high heat before cooking in slow cooker.

As a broad generalization, most foods you cook in the slow cooker will take twice as long to cook on the low setting as on the high setting.

Hasty Hash Browns

1 (32 ounce) package frozen hash-brown potatoes, thawed
1 (8 ounce) package shredded sharp cheddar cheese
1 (8 ounce) carton fresh whole mushrooms, sliced
1 (16 ounce) package frozen chopped bell peppers and
   onions, thawed
1 teaspoon seasoned salt
1 (10 ounce) can cream of mushroom soup

■ Combine potatoes, cheese, mushrooms, bell peppers and
  onions, and seasoned salt in sprayed slow cooker. Heat
  soup with ¼ cup water to thin and pour over potatoes.

■ Cover and cook on LOW for 7 to 9 hours or on HIGH for
  4 hours. Stir gently before serving. Serves 8.

Slow cookers work best when filled
to between two-thirds and three-
fourths of capacity. Filling a cooker
to the brim will prevent even cooking and
will require a longer cooking time.

Cheezy Potatoes

**1 (28 ounce) bag frozen diced potatoes with onions and
    peppers, thawed**
**1 (8 ounce) package shredded Monterey Jack and cheddar
    cheese blend**
1 (10 ounce) can cream of celery soup
1 (8 ounce) carton sour cream

- Combine potatoes, cheese, soup, sour cream and
  1 teaspoon pepper in sprayed slow cooker and mix well.
  Cover and cook on LOW 4 to 6 hours. Stir well before
  serving. Serves 6 to 8.

Not only is the slow cooker a
convenience and a time-saver, it saves
energy because it uses very little
electricity. When cooking on the low
setting, the slow cooker will use less
energy than most light bulbs.

Thanksgiving Sweet Potatoes

2 (20 ounce) cans sweet potatoes, drained, mashed
½ cup (1 stick) plus ⅓ cup (⅔ stick) butter, divided
¼ cup sugar
¼ cup plus ⅓ cup packed brown sugar, divided
2 eggs, slightly beaten
½ cup milk
⅓ cup chopped pecans
3 tablespoons flour

■ Combine mashed sweet potatoes, ½ cup melted butter, sugar and ¼ cup brown sugar in large bowl and mix well. Stir in beaten eggs and milk and spoon into sprayed slow cooker.

■ Combine remaining melted butter, pecans, flour and remaining brown sugar in bowl and sprinkle over sweet potato mixture. Cover and cook on HIGH for 3 to 4 hours. Serves 8.

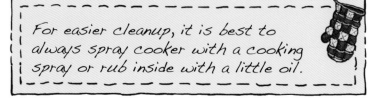

For easier cleanup, it is best to always spray cooker with a cooking spray or rub inside with a little oil.

Creamed Spinach

2 (10 ounce) packages frozen chopped spinach, thawed
1 (16 ounce) carton small curd cottage cheese
1½ cups shredded American or cheddar cheese
3 eggs, beaten
¼ cup (½ stick) butter, melted
¼ cup flour

■ Drain spinach and squeeze between paper towels to completely remove excess moisture.

■ Combine all ingredients in bowl and mix well. Spoon into sprayed slow cooker. Cover and cook on HIGH for 1 hour, reduce heat to LOW and cook for additional 3 to 5 hours or until knife inserted in center comes out clean. Serves 4 to 6.

Families are like fudge... mostly sweet with a few nuts.

Spinach-Artichoke Special

2 (16 ounce) packages frozen chopped spinach,
**   thawed, drained**
1 onion, chopped
1 red bell pepper, seeded, chopped
¼ cup (½ stick) butter, melted
1 cup shredded Italian cheese
⅓ cup seasoned breadcrumbs
1 teaspoon seasoned salt
1 (14 ounce) can artichokes, drained, chopped
1 (10 ounce) can cream of celery soup
¾ cup shredded parmesan cheese

- Squeeze spinach between paper towels to completely remove excess moisture.

- Combine spinach, onion, bell pepper, butter, cheese, breadcrumbs, seasoned salt and artichokes in sprayed slow cooker.

- Heat soup and ¼ cup water in saucepan to thin and pour over vegetables. Cover and cook on LOW for 5 to 7 hours.

- Sprinkle with parmesan cheese just before serving. Serves 8 to 10.

Zucchini-Squash Combo

1½ pounds small yellow squash, peeled, cubed
1½ pounds zucchini, peeled, cubed
1 teaspoon seasoned salt
¼ cup (½ stick) butter, melted
½ cup seasoned breadcrumbs
½ cup shredded cheddar cheese

■ Place squash in sprayed slow cooker and sprinkle with seasoned salt and pepper.

■ Pour melted butter over squash and sprinkle with breadcrumbs and cheese. Cover and cook on LOW for 5 to 6 hours. Serves 6 to 8.

Slow cookers meld flavors deliciously, but colors can fade over long cooking times, therefore you can "dress up" your dish with colorful garnishes such as fresh parsley or chives, salsas, extra shredded cheeses, and a sprinkle of paprika or a dollop of sour cream.

Garden Casserole

1 pound yellow squash, sliced
1 pound zucchini, sliced
1 green bell pepper, seeded, chopped
1 red bell pepper, seeded, chopped
3 ribs celery, sliced
2 (10 ounce) cans cream of chicken soup
½ cup (1 stick) plus 3 tablespoons butter
1 (6 ounce) box herb stuffing mix

- Combine squash, zucchini, bell peppers and celery in large bowl; gently stir until soup mixes with vegetables.

- Melt ½ cup butter in skillet and add stuffing mix; mix well and set aside 1 cup for topping. Stir into vegetable-soup mixture and spoon into sprayed slow cooker. Cover and cook on LOW for 3 to 5 hours.

- Reheat the stuffing in skillet and sprinkle over top of vegetables. Drizzle 3 tablespoons melted butter over top; serve immediately. Serves 8 to 10.

Creamy Rice Casserole

2 (6 ounce) boxes long grain-wild rice mix
1 (10 ounce) can cream of chicken soup
½ cup (1 stick) butter, melted
1 (10 ounce) package frozen chopped bell peppers and
**   onions, thawed**
3 ribs celery, thinly sliced
1 (4 ounce) can diced pimentos
1 (8 ounce) package shredded Velveeta® cheese

- Place rice mix, contents of seasoning packet, butter, bell peppers and onions, celery, pimentos and cheese in sprayed slow cooker.

- Heat soup and 2½ cups water in saucepan and stir to thin. Pour over rice and stir.

- Cover and cook on LOW for 6 to 10 hours or on HIGH for 2 to 3 hours 30 minutes. Serves 6 to 8.

The more complex the shape of a pasta, the better a sauce or seasoning will cling to its ridges and grooves, nooks and crannies.

Autumn Rice Bake

1 cup brown rice
1½ cups orange juice
1 apple, peeled, cored, chopped
⅓ cup Craisins®
⅓ cup chopped pecans
2 tablespoons brown sugar
½ teaspoon ground cinnamon

- Place rice, orange juice, apple, Craisins®, pecans, brown sugar, cinnamon and ½ teaspoon salt in sprayed slow cooker. Cover and cook on LOW for 4 to 5 hours. Serves 4.

Carnival Couscous

1 (5.7 ounce) box herbed-chicken couscous
1 red bell pepper, seeded, julienned
1 green bell pepper, seeded, julienned
2 small yellow squash, sliced
1 (16 ounce) package frozen mixed vegetables, thawed
1 (10 ounce) can French onion soup
¼ cup (½ stick) butter, melted
½ teaspoon seasoned salt

- Combine all ingredients with 1½ cups water in sprayed slow cooker and mix well. Cover and cook on LOW for 2 to 4 hours. Serves 4.

Creamy Spinach Noodles

1 (12 ounce) package medium noodles
1 cup half-and-half cream
1 (10 ounce) package frozen chopped spinach, thawed
6 tablespoons (¾ stick) butter, melted
2 teaspoons seasoned salt
1½ cups shredded cheddar-Monterey Jack cheese

- Cook noodles according to package directions and drain. Place in sprayed slow cooker. Add half-and-half cream, spinach, butter and seasoned salt and stir until they blend well. Cover and cook on LOW for 2 to 3 hours.

- When ready to serve, fold in cheese. Serves 4.

What's the difference between pasta and noodles? Noodles are made with durum flour (more finely ground than semolina), water and eggs. Eggs are a required ingredient. All other forms of pasta are made from semolina flour and water and are generically referred to as macaroni.

Tomato-Artichoke Pasta

3 (15 ounce) cans Italian stewed tomatoes, divided
2 (14 ounce) cans artichoke hearts, drained, quartered
1 teaspoon minced garlic
1 (5 ounce) can evaporated milk
1 (12 ounce) package penne pasta
1 cup grated parmesan cheese

- Drain 2 cans of tomatoes and place in sprayed slow cooker. Add tomatoes with liquid, artichoke hearts and garlic.

- Cover and cook on LOW for 6 to 8 hours or on HIGH for 3 to 4 hours.

- Stir in evaporated milk and let stand covered for about 10 minutes. Cook pasta according to package directions, drain and place on serving plate. Serve artichoke mixture over pasta and sprinkle each serving with a little parmesan cheese. Serves 6.

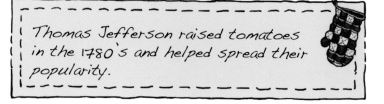

Thomas Jefferson raised tomatoes in the 1780's and helped spread their popularity.

Main Dishes

Chicken

Beef

Pork

Seafood

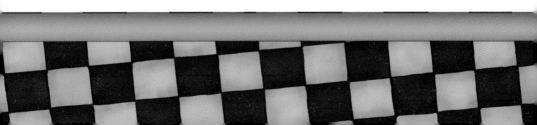

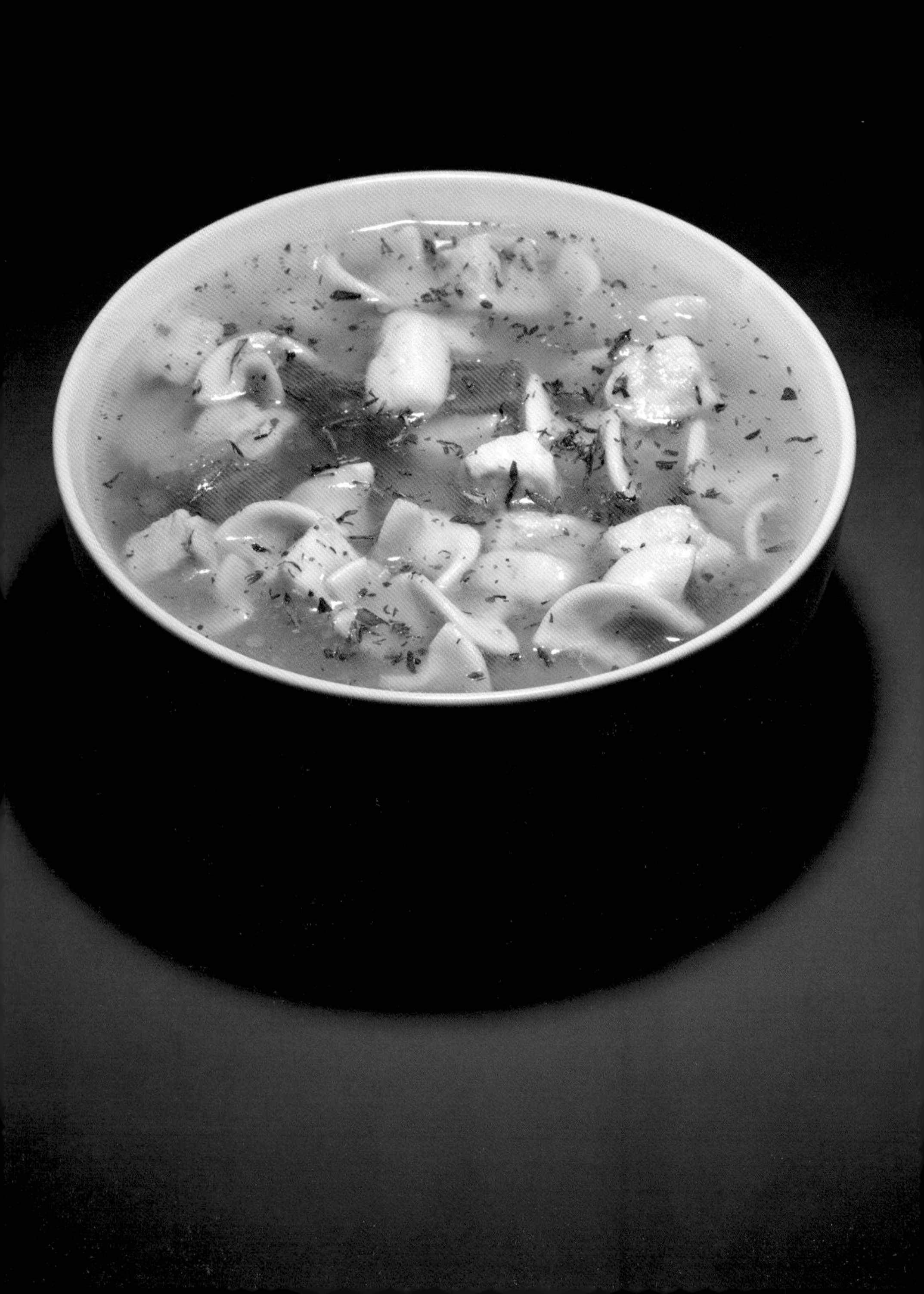

Quick Chicken-Noodle Soup

2 (14 ounce) cans chicken broth
2 boneless, skinless chicken breast halves, cubed
1 (8 ounce) can sliced carrots, drained
2 ribs celery, sliced
½ (8 ounce) package medium egg noodles

- Combine broth, chicken, carrots, celery and generous dash of pepper in large saucepan. Boil and cook for 3 minutes.

- Stir in noodles, reduce heat and cook for 10 minutes or until noodles are done; stir often. Serves 4 to 6.

Chicken noodle soup is the most popular soup.

Easy Chicken-Rice Soup

8 boneless, skinless chicken breast halves, cooked
2 (14 ounce) cans chicken broth
1 cup sliced carrots
1 cup rice

- Cut cooked chicken into small pieces and place in large saucepan.

- Add chicken broth, carrots, rice, 1 teaspoon salt and ¼ teaspoon pepper and simmer for about 35 minutes or until rice is tender. Serves 6.

Oriental Chicken-Noodle Soup

1 (3 ounce) package chicken-flavor ramen noodles
1 rotisserie chicken, boned, skinned, cubed
2 medium stalks bok choy with leaves, thinly sliced
1 (8 ounce) can sliced carrots, drained
1 red bell pepper, seeded, chopped

- Break apart noodles, place in 3 cups water and heat in soup pot. Stir in chicken, bok choy, carrots and bell pepper.

- Bring to boil, reduce heat and simmer for 3 minutes; stir occasionally. Stir in flavor packet from noodles and serve immediately. Serves 8.

Zesty Creamy Chicken Soup

Can you open cans? Don't be put off by
the number of ingredients in this recipe.

2 tablespoons butter
½ onion, finely chopped
1 (10 ounce) can cream of mushroom soup
2 (10 ounce) cans cream of chicken soup
1 (14 ounce) can chicken broth
2 soup cans milk
1 (16 ounce) package, cubed Mexican Velveeta® cheese
4 boneless, skinless chicken breast halves, cooked, diced

■ Melt butter in large saucepan or roasting pan and saute
onion for 10 minutes, but do not brown. Add remaining
ingredients and heat but do not boil.

■ Reduce heat to low, cook until cheese melts and stir
constantly. Serve piping hot. Serves 8.

TIP: This is really the "easy" way to make chicken soup
and if you are in an absolute rush, you could even use
2 (12 ounce) cans chicken. Leftover turkey could be
substituted for chicken.

Anytime Chicken-Broccoli Chowder

2 (14 ounce) cans chicken broth
1 (10 ounce) package frozen chopped broccoli
1½ cups dry mashed potato flakes
2½ cups cooked, cut-up chicken breasts
1 (8 ounce) package shredded mozzarella cheese
1 (8 ounce) carton whipping cream
1 cup milk

■ Combine broth and broccoli in large saucepan. Bring to boil, reduce heat, cover and simmer for 5 minutes.

■ Stir in dry potato flakes and mix until they blend well. Add chicken, cheese, cream, milk, 1 cup water and a little salt and pepper.

■ Heat over medium heat and stir occasionally until hot and cheese melts, for about 5 minutes. Serves 8.

TIP: Garnish with chopped green onions.

Whipped Chicken Chowder

3 cups cooked, cubed chicken
1 (14 ounce) can chicken broth
2 (10 ounce) cans cream of potato soup
1 large onion, chopped
3 ribs celery, sliced diagonally
1 (16 ounce) package frozen whole kernel corn, thawed
⅔ cup whipping cream

- Combine all ingredients except cream in large soup pot with ¾ cup water.

- Cover and cook on low heat for about 45 minutes. Add whipping cream and heat for additional 10 minutes on low. Do not boil. Serves 6.

Chowders contain any of several
varieties of seafood and vegetables.
New England-style chowder is made
with milk or cream and Manhattan-style
chowder is made with tomatoes.

La Placita Enchilada Soup

6 boneless, skinless chicken breast halves
½ cup (1 stick) butter
2 cloves garlic, minced
1 onion, minced
⅓ cup flour
1 (15 ounce) can Mexican stewed tomatoes, chopped
1 (7 ounce) can diced green chilies
1 (1 pint) carton sour cream
1 (8 ounce) package shredded cheddar cheese

■ Cook chicken with 12 cups water in large saucepan until tender. Reserve broth, cube chicken and set aside. Melt butter in large roasting pan and cook garlic and onion until tender.

■ Add 1 teaspoon salt to flour in bowl, slowly pour flour into butter mixture and stir constantly to dissolve all lumps.

■ Continue stirring and slowly pour in reserved chicken broth. Cook until soup thickens to desired consistency.

■ Add chicken, tomatoes, green chilies and sour cream. Mix well and heat. Serve in individual bowls and sprinkle with cheese. Serves 6.

Chicken and Rice Mambo Gumbo

3 (14 ounce) cans chicken broth
1 pound boneless, skinless chicken breasts, cubed
2 (15 ounce) cans whole kernel corn, drained
2 (15 ounce) cans stewed tomatoes with liquid
¾ cup white rice
2 tablespoons Cajun seasoning
2 (10 ounce) packages frozen okra, thawed, chopped

■ Combine chicken broth and chicken in soup pot and cook on high heat for 15 minutes.

■ Add remaining ingredients and 1 teaspoon pepper and bring to boil Reduce heat and simmer for 30 minutes or until rice is done. Serves 8.

Rice came to the South by way of a storm-ravaged, merchant ship sailing from Madagascar and reaching the port of Charleston for safe haven. As a gift to the people, the ship's captain gave a local planter some "Golden Seed Rice" and by 1700, rice was a major crop in the colonies.

Creamy Chicken-Spinach Soup

1 (9 ounce) package refrigerated cheese tortellini, optional
2 (14 ounce) cans chicken broth, divided
1 (10 ounce) can cream of chicken soup
1 (12 ounce) can white chicken meat with liquid
1 (10 ounce) package frozen chopped spinach
2 cups milk

■ Cook tortellini in soup pot with 1 can chicken broth according to package directions.

■ Stir in remaining can broth, soup, chicken, spinach, milk, 1 teaspoon salt and ½ teaspoon pepper. Bring to boil, reduce heat to low and simmer for 10 minutes. Serves 8.

TIP: Adding the cheese tortellini makes this a heartier soup.

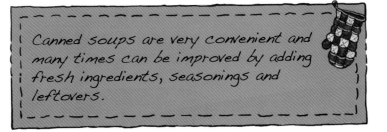

Canned soups are very convenient and many times can be improved by adding fresh ingredients, seasonings and leftovers.

Cheesy Chicken Chili

1 (28 ounce) can diced or stewed tomatoes
1 (15 ounce) can kidney beans, rinsed, drained
1 (15 ounce) can pinto beans, drained
2 (14 ounce) cans chicken broth
2 (12 ounce) cans chicken breasts with liquid
1 tablespoon chili powder
1 (8 ounce) package shredded Mexican 4-cheese
    blend, divided

- Combine tomatoes, kidney beans, pinto beans, broth, chicken, chili powder and a little salt and pepper in soup pot.

- Bring to a boil, reduce heat and simmer for 25 minutes.

- Stir in half cheese and spoon into individual soup bowls. Sprinkle remaining cheese on top of each serving. Serves 8.

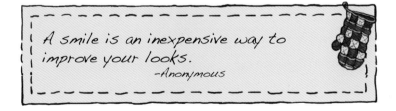

A smile is an inexpensive way to improve your looks.
                    —Anonymous

White Lightning Chili

1½ cups dried navy, kidney or pinto beans
3 (14 ounce) cans chicken broth
2 tablespoons butter
1 onion, chopped
3 cups cooked, chopped chicken
1½ teaspoons ground cumin
1 teaspoon cayenne pepper

- Sort and wash beans, cover with water and soak overnight. Drain beans and place in soup pot and add broth, butter, 1 cup water and onion.

- Bring to boil, reduce heat and cover. Simmer for 2 hours and stir occasionally.

- With potato masher, mash half of beans in soup pot. Add chicken, cumin and cayenne pepper. Bring to a boil, reduce heat and cover. Simmer for additional 30 minutes. Serves 6 to 8.

TIP: Line serving bowls with flour tortillas. Spoon in chili and top with shredded Monterey Jack cheese.

Pepe's Tortilla Soup

*Don't let the number of ingredients keep
you from serving this. It's really easy.*

**3 large boneless, skinless chicken breast halves,
      cooked, chopped**
1 (10 ounce) package frozen corn, thawed
1 onion, chopped
3 (14 ounce) cans chicken broth
2 (10 ounce) cans diced tomatoes and green chilies
2 teaspoons ground cumin
2 teaspoons chili powder
1 clove garlic, minced
6 corn tortillas

■ Combine all ingredients except tortillas in large soup pot.
  Bring to boil, reduce heat and simmer for 35 minutes.

■ Preheat oven to 350°F (175°C).

■ While soup simmers, cut tortillas into 1-inch strips and place
  on baking sheet. Bake for about 5 minutes or until crisp.
  Serve tortilla strips with each serving of soup. Serves 6.

Steaming Broccoli-Rice Soup

1 (6 ounce) package chicken and wild rice mix
1 (10 ounce) package frozen chopped broccoli
2 (10 ounce) cans cream of chicken soup
1 (12 ounce) can chicken breast chunks

■ Combine rice mix, contents of seasoning packet and 5 cups water in soup pot. Bring to boil, reduce heat and simmer for 15 minutes.

■ Stir in broccoli, chicken soup and chicken. Cover and simmer for additional 5 minutes. Serves 8.

Frozen vegetables take less time to cook than fresh vegetables. When you are in a hurry, frozen vegetables are the way to go.

Cold Night Bean Dinner

1½ cups dried navy beans
3 (14 ounce) cans chicken broth
¼ cup (½ stick) butter
1 onion, chopped
1 clove garlic, minced
3 cups chopped, cooked chicken
1½ teaspoons ground cumin
2 teaspoons cayenne pepper
Shredded Monterey Jack cheese

■ Sort, wash beans and place in soup pot. Cover with water 2 inches above beans and soak overnight.

■ Drain beans and add broth, butter, 1 cup water, onion and garlic. Bring to boil, reduce heat and cover. Simmer for 2 hours and stir occasionally. Add more water if needed.

■ With potato masher, mash half beans. Add chicken, cumin and cayenne pepper. Bring to boil, reduce heat and cover. Simmer for additional 30 minutes.

■ When ready to serve, spoon in bowls and top with 1 to 2 tablespoons cheese. Serves 8.

Hearty Chicken-Rice Stew

2 (12 ounce) cans white chicken meat with liquid
2 (14 ounce) cans chicken broth
1 (15 ounce) can Mexican stewed tomatoes
2 (10 ounce) packages frozen seasoning blend, thawed*
2 cups instant white or brown rice
1 (15 ounce) can whole kernel corn
1 teaspoon chili powder

■ Combine chicken, broth, stewed tomatoes, seasoning blend
and rice in heavy soup pot. Bring to a boil, reduce heat and
simmer for 10 minutes.

■ Stir in corn, chili powder, and a little salt and pepper.
Bring to a boil, reduce heat and simmer for 5 minutes.
Serves 6 to 8.

*TIP: Look for frozen seasoning blend in the frozen vegetable
section. It is generally a combination of chopped onions,
green and red bell peppers, celery and parsley.

There are four cities in the United
States that have the word "chicken"
in their names: Chicken, Alaska;
Chicken Bristle, Illinois; Chicken
Bristle, Kentucky; and Chicken Town,
Pennsylvania.

Chicken-Sausage Stew

1 (16 ounce) package frozen stew vegetables
2 (12 ounce) cans chicken breast with liquid
½ pound hot Italian sausage, sliced
2 (15 ounce) cans Italian stewed tomatoes
1 (14 ounce) can chicken broth
1 cup cooked instant rice

■ Combine all ingredients except rice and add a little salt in large heavy soup pot. Bring to boil, reduce heat and simmer for 25 minutes.

■ Stir in cooked rice during last 5 minutes of cooking time. Serves 8.

Many countries serve soup for breakfast. Breakfast in Japan starts with miso soup, fish broth with rice. Breakfast in France often starts with leftover soup.

Smoked Turkey Stampede

2 tablespoons olive oil
1 small onion, chopped
1 green bell pepper, seeded, chopped
1 (14 ounce) can chicken broth
1 medium potato, peeled, cubed
1 pound smoked turkey kielbasa, sliced
1 (15 ounce) can great northern beans with liquid

- Combine oil, onion and bell pepper in soup pot and cook for 5 minutes. Stir in broth, potato, turkey kielbasa, 1 cup water and a little salt and pepper.

- Bring to boil, reduce heat to medium and simmer for 15 minutes or until potato is tender.

- Stir in beans and heat just until soup is thoroughly hot. Serves 6.

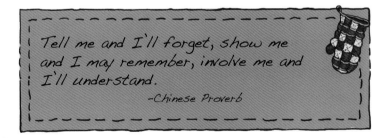

Tell me and I'll forget, show me and I may remember, involve me and I'll understand.

−Chinese Proverb

Hearty 15-Minute Turkey Soup

This is great served with cornbread.

1 (14 ounce) can chicken broth
3 (15 ounce) cans navy beans with liquid
1 (28 ounce) can Italian stewed tomatoes
     with liquid
3 cups cooked, cubed white turkey
2 teaspoons minced garlic
1 (6 ounce) package baby spinach, stems removed

- Combine broth, beans, stewed tomatoes, turkey, garlic and a little salt and pepper in soup pot.

- Bring to boil, reduce heat and simmer on medium heat for about 10 minutes.

- Stir in baby spinach, boil and cook, stirring constantly for 5 minutes. Serves 8.

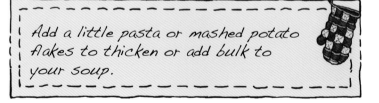

Add a little pasta or mashed potato flakes to thicken or add bulk to your soup.

Turkey with Avocado

3 large potatoes, peeled, cubed
2 (14 ounce) cans chicken broth
1 teaspoon ground thyme
½ pound smoked turkey breast, cubed
1 (10 ounce) package frozen corn
3 slices bacon, cooked crisp, drained
1 large avocado
4 plum tomatoes, coarsely chopped
1 lime

- Combine potatoes, broth and thyme in soup pot, cover and bring to boil Reduce heat and simmer until potatoes are tender, for about 20 minutes.

- With slotted spoon transfer half of potatoes to blender or food processor, puree and pour into soup pot. Add turkey and corn and simmer for 5 minutes.

- Crumble bacon; peel and slice avocado. Add bacon, avocado, tomatoes, juice of lime and a little salt and pepper to turkey mixture. Stir gently to mix. Serves 8.

TIP: Peel and cut avocado just before serving to prevent discoloration.

Tasty Turkey-Veggie Brew

2 (14 ounce) cans chicken broth
2 teaspoons minced garlic
1 (16 ounce) package frozen corn
1 (10 ounce) package frozen cut green beans
1 (10 ounce) package frozen sliced carrots
2 (15 ounce) cans Italian stewed tomatoes
2½ cups cooked, cubed turkey
1 cup shredded mozzarella cheese

■ Combine broth, 1 cup water, garlic, corn, green beans, carrots, tomatoes, turkey and 1 teaspoon salt in large, heavy soup pot. (Add shell pasta, if desired.)

■ Bring to boil, reduce heat and simmer for 15 minutes. Before serving, top each bowl of soup with mozzarella cheese. Serves 8.

True friends are those who really know you but love you anyway.
    —Edna Buchanan

Cream of Turkey Blend

1 (10 ounce) can cream of celery soup
1 (10 ounce) can cream of chicken soup
2 soup cans milk
1 cup cooked, finely diced turkey

■ Combine all ingredients in large saucepan.

■ Serve hot. Serves 4.

The Campbell Soup Company began in 1868 as a canning company. One of its chemist/owners developed condensed soup in 1897 and it won a gold medal at the Paris Exposition in 1900. The medal insignia continues to be on some of its labels today.

Turkey Tango

3 - 4 cups chopped turkey
2 (14 ounce) cans chicken broth
2 (10 ounce) cans diced tomatoes and green chilies
1 (15 ounce) can whole kernel corn, drained
1 large onion, chopped
1 (10 ounce) can tomato soup
3 tablespoons cornstarch

■ Combine turkey, broth, tomatoes and green chilies, corn, onion and tomato soup in large roasting pan.

■ Mix cornstarch with 3 tablespoons water and add to soup mixture.

■ Bring mixture to a boil, reduce heat and simmer for 2 hours. Stir occasionally. Serves 6 to 8.

If you have any leftover cooked pasta, meat or vegetables, use them for soup ingredients. Most cooked vegetables can also be pureed and stirred in to thicken soups.

All-American Soup

3 boneless, skinless chicken breast halves, cut into strips
1 onion, chopped
1 (10 ounce) can diced tomatoes and green chilies
2 large baking potatoes, peeled, cubed
2 (14 ounce) cans chicken broth
1 (10 ounce) can cream of celery soup
1 cup milk
1 teaspoon dried basil
1 (8 ounce) package shredded Velveeta® cheese
½ cup sour cream

■ Place chicken strips, onion, tomatoes and green chilies, potatoes, milk and basil in sprayed slow cooker. Heat broth and soup in saucepan to thin and pour over vegetables.

■ Cover and cook on LOW for 6 to 8 hours.

■ Stir in cheese and sour cream. Cover and cook for additional 10 to 15 minutes or just until cheese melts. Serves 6 to 8.

TIP: You can leave out the 2 cans of broth and serve this chicken dish over hot cooked rice topped with about 1 cup of lightly crushed potato chips.

Confetti Chicken Soup

1 pound boneless, skinless chicken thighs
1 (6 ounce) package chicken and herb-flavored rice
3 (14 ounce) cans chicken broth
3 carrots, peeled, sliced
1 (10 ounce) can cream of chicken soup
1½ tablespoons chicken seasoning
1 (10 ounce) package frozen corn, thawed
1 (10 ounce) package frozen cut green beans or baby
    green peas, thawed

- Cut thighs in thin strips.

- Combine chicken, rice, chicken broth, carrots, soup, chicken seasoning and 1 cup water in sprayed 5 to 6-quart slow cooker.

- Cover and cook on LOW for 8 to 9 hours.

- About 30 minutes before serving, turn heat to HIGH and add corn and green beans (or peas) to cooker. Continue cooking for additional 30 minutes. Serves 6.

Once the dish is cooked and served, do not keep in cooker too long to avoid development of harmful bacteria. Remove remaining food and refrigerate. Do not heat leftovers in the slow cooker.

Chicken Stew

1½ - 2 pounds boneless, skinless chicken thighs
1 (16 ounce) package frozen stew vegetables
1 (1 ounce) packet dry vegetable soup mix
1¼ cups pearl barley
2 (14 ounce) cans chicken broth

- Combine all ingredients plus 1 teaspoon each of salt and pepper and 4 cups water in sprayed large slow cooker.

- Cover and cook on LOW for 5 to 6 hours or on HIGH for 3 hours. Serves 6.

A team of scientists at the University of Nebraska confirmed what grandmothers have known for centuries - chicken soup is good for colds. Chicken soup contains several anti-inflammatory ingredients that affect the immune system.

Tortellini Soup

1 (1 ounce) packet white sauce mix
3 boneless, skinless chicken breast halves
1 (14 ounce) can chicken broth
1 teaspoon minced garlic
1 tablespoon dried basil
1 (8 ounce) package cheese tortellini
1½ cups half-and-half cream
1 (10 ounce) package fresh baby spinach

■ Place white sauce mix in sprayed 5 to 6-quart slow cooker. Add 4 cups water and stir until mixture is smooth.

■ Cut chicken into 1-inch pieces. Add chicken, broth, garlic, basil, 1 teaspoon salt and 1 teaspoon pepper to mixture.

■ Cover and cook on LOW for 6 to 7 hours or on HIGH for 3 hours.

■ Stir in tortellini, cover and cook 1 hour more on HIGH. Stir in half-and-half cream and fresh spinach and cook just enough for soup to get hot. Serves 6.

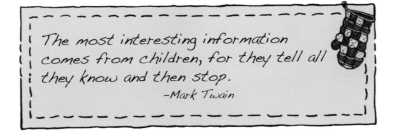

The most interesting information comes from children, for they tell all they know and then stop.
—Mark Twain

White Chicken Chili

1½ pounds boneless, skinless chicken thighs
3 (15 ounce) cans great northern beans, rinsed, drained
1 (15 ounce) can white hominy, drained
1 (1 ounce) packet taco seasoning
1 (7 ounce) can diced green chilies
1 (10 ounce) can cream of chicken soup
1 (8 ounce) carton sour cream
Chopped green onions

- Place chicken in sprayed slow cooker and top with beans, hominy, taco seasoning and green chilies. Heat chicken soup in saucepan to thin and pour over chicken.

- Cover and cook on LOW for 8 to 10 hours.

- Before serving, stir vigorously to break up chicken pieces. Place 1 tablespoon sour cream and few pieces green onions on top of each serving. Serves 6.

You can thicken liquid in the slow cooker by mixing 1 tablespoon cornstarch with 2 tablespoons cold water. Add to liquid and cook until liquid reaches gravy or sauce consistency.

Southwestern Chicken Pot

6 boneless, skinless chicken breast halves
1 teaspoon ground cumin
1 teaspoon chili powder
1 (10 ounce) can cream of chicken soup
1 (10 ounce) can fiesta nacho cheese soup
1 cup salsa
Rice or noodles, cooked
Flour tortillas

- Sprinkle chicken breasts with cumin, chili powder, and a little salt and pepper and place in sprayed oval slow cooker.

- Combine soups and salsa in saucepan. Heat just enough to mix well and pour over chicken breasts. Cover and cook on LOW for 6 to 7 hours. Serve over rice or noodles with warmed flour tortillas spread with butter. Serves 4 to 6.

Some flavors, such as chili powder and garlic, will become more intense during cooking. Others tend to "cook out" and lose their flavor. It is always wise to taste at the end of cooking and season as needed.

Old-Time Chicken Soup

6 boneless, skinless chicken thighs, cut into 1-inch pieces
3 (14 ounce) cans chicken broth
1 carrot, sliced
2 ribs celery, sliced
1 onion, chopped
1 (15 ounce) can stewed tomatoes
1 (8 ounce) can green peas, drained
1 teaspoon dried thyme
½ cup elbow macaroni

- Combine chicken pieces, broth, carrot, celery, onion, tomatoes, peas, thyme and 1 teaspoon each of salt and pepper in sprayed slow cooker.

- Cover and cook on LOW for 6 hours 30 minutes to 7 hours.

- Increase heat to HIGH, add macaroni, cover and cook for additional 30 minutes. Serves 6.

Fresh herbs provide a more authentic flavor; however, dried herbs may be substituted in any of our recipes. As a general rule, dried herbs are more potent. If using dried herbs, reduce the required amount by half.

Curly Noodle Soup

6 - 7 boneless, skinless chicken thighs
1 (16 ounce) package baby carrots, halved
1 (8 ounce) can sliced bamboo shoots, drained
1 (8 ounce) can sliced water chestnuts, drained
1 (3 ounce) package Oriental-flavor ramen noodle
    soup mix
1 (32 ounce) carton chicken broth
2 tablespoons butter, melted
1 (10 ounce) package frozen green peas, thawed, drained

- Layer chicken thighs, carrots, bamboo shoots, water chestnuts, seasoning packet from noodles, broth and butter in sprayed slow cooker. Cover and cook on LOW for 7 to 8 hours.

- Remove chicken thighs with slotted spoon and shred with 2 forks. Return chicken to slow cooker and add peas and noodles; cover and cook for additional 10 minutes or until noodles are tender. Serves 6.

When I was a boy of 14, my father was so ignorant I could hardly stand to have the old man around. But when I got to be 21, I was astonished at how much the old man had learned in seven years.

—Mark Twain

Chicken-Barley Soup

1½ - 2 pounds boneless, skinless chicken thighs
1 (16 ounce) package frozen stew vegetables
1 (1 ounce) packet dry vegetable soup mix
1¼ cups pearl barley
3 (14 ounce) cans chicken broth

- Combine all ingredients with 1 teaspoon each of salt and pepper and 4 cups water in large, sprayed slow cooker.

- Cover and cook on LOW for 5 to 6 hours or on HIGH for 3 hours. Serves 6 to 8.

Lucky Chicken Soup

3 cups cooked, cubed chicken
1 (15 ounce) can stewed tomatoes
1 (10 ounce) can enchilada sauce
1 onion, chopped
1 teaspoon minced garlic
1 (14 ounce) can chicken broth
1 (15 ounce) can whole kernel corn
1 teaspoon chili powder

- Combine chicken, tomatoes, enchilada sauce, onion, garlic, broth, corn, chili powder and 2 cups water in sprayed slow cooker. Cover and cook on LOW for 6 to 8 hours or on HIGH for 3 to 4 hours. Serves 8.

Monterey Bake

6 (6 inch) corn tortillas
3 cups cubed cooked chicken
1 (10 ounce) package frozen whole kernel corn
1 (15 ounce) can pinto beans with liquid
1 (16 ounce) jar hot salsa
¼ cup sour cream
1 tablespoon flour
3 tablespoons snipped fresh cilantro
1 (8 ounce) package shredded 4-cheese blend

- Preheat oven to 250°F (120°C).

- Cut tortillas into 6 wedges. Place half of tortilla wedges in sprayed slow cooker. Place remaining wedges on baking pan, bake for about 10 minutes and set aside.

- Layer chicken, corn and beans over tortillas in cooker. Combine salsa, sour cream, flour and cilantro in bowl and pour over chicken, corn and beans. Cover and cook on LOW for 3 to 4 hours.

- When ready to serve, place baked tortillas wedges and cheese on top of each serving. Serves 4 to 6.

Aloha Chicken

3 pounds boneless skinless chicken breast halves
1 (8 ounce) can crushed pineapple
1 tablespoon soy sauce
2 tablespoons mustard
1 cup packed brown sugar
½ cup (1 stick) butter, melted
½ cup lemon juice
½ cup honey

■ Place all ingredients in sprayed slow cooker. Cover and cook on LOW for 4 to 5 hours, or until chicken is thoroughly cooked. Serves 8.

A "free-range" chicken is one that is given twice as much room as mass produced chickens and they are free to roam indoors and outdoors. This is supposed to enhance the "chicken" flavor because they are "happy" chickens.

Chicken-Veggie Surprise

3 (14 ounce) can chicken broth
1 (15 ounce) can sliced carrots, drained
1 (15 ounce) can green peas, drained
1 red or yellow bell pepper, seeded, chopped
1 teaspoon dried parsley
2 cups cooked, cubed chicken
1 (16 ounce) package frozen broccoli florets
4 ounces pasta

■ Combine broth, carrots, peas, bell pepper, parsley, chicken
   and broccoli in sprayed slow cooker. Cover and cook on
   LOW for 5 to 7 hours.

■ Stir in pasta, cover and cook for additional 1 hour. Serves
   6 to 8.

*TIP: For a heartier soup, add additional 4 ounces pasta and
   1/4 cup each of sliced mushrooms and tomatoes.*

Supreme Sun-Dried Chicken

3 pounds boneless, skinless chicken breast halves
1 tablespoon canola oil
1 teaspoon minced garlic
½ cup white wine (can use cooking wine)
1 (14 ounce) can chicken broth
1 teaspoon dried basil
¾ cup chopped sun-dried tomatoes
1 (10 ounce) box couscous

■ Cut chicken into 8 to 9 serving pieces. Heat oil in large
skillet and brown several pieces at a time, making sure
pieces brown evenly. Place each browned piece of chicken
in sprayed large slow cooker.

■ Add garlic, wine, broth and basil to skillet and bring to a
boil. Pour over chicken and scatter tomatoes on top. Cover
and cook on LOW for 4 to 6 hours.

■ Cook couscous according to package directions and place
on serving platter. Place chicken pieces on top of couscous.
Serve sauce on the side. Serves 8.

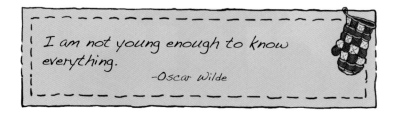

*I am not young enough to know
everything.*
—Oscar Wilde

Lemon-Herb Chicken Pasta

1 pound chicken tenders
Lemon-herb chicken seasoning
3 tablespoons butter
1 onion, coarsely chopped
1 (15 ounce) can diced tomatoes
1 (10 ounce) can golden mushroom soup
(8 ounce) box angel hair pasta

- Pat chicken tenders dry with paper towels and sprinkle with ample amount of chicken seasoning. Melt butter in large skillet, brown chicken and place in sprayed oval slow cooker. Pour remaining butter and seasonings over chicken and cover with onion.

- Combine tomatoes and soup in bowl and pour over chicken and onion. Cover and cook on LOW for 4 to 5 hours.

- Cook pasta according to package directions. Serve chicken and sauce over pasta. Serves 4.

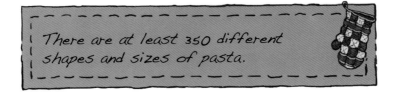

There are at least 350 different shapes and sizes of pasta.

Pizza-Parmesan Chicken

1 large egg, beaten
1 cup seasoned breadcrumbs
2 tablespoons canola oil
6 boneless, skinless chicken breast halves
1 (10 ounce) jar pizza sauce
⅔ cup grated parmesan cheese
6 slices mozzarella cheese

- Place egg in shallow bowl. In separate shallow bowl, place breadcrumbs. Dip chicken breasts into egg and then into breadcrumbs. Press crumbs on all sides of chicken. Heat oil in large skillet and saute chicken.

- Arrange one layer of chicken in sprayed slow cooker and pour half pizza sauce on top. Add second layer of chicken and pour remaining sauce over top. Cover and cook on LOW for 6 to 8 hours or just until chicken is tender but not dry.

- Sprinkle with parmesan cheese and add mozzarella slices on top; cover and cook for additional 15 minutes. Serves 6.

Rolled Chicken Florentine

6 boneless, skinless chicken breast halves
6 thin slices ham
6 slices Swiss cheese
**1 (10 ounce) package frozen chopped spinach, thawed,
    well drained***
1 (16 ounce) package baby carrots
2 (10 ounce) cans cream of chicken soup
1 (10 ounce) box chicken-flavored rice

- With flat side of meat mallet, pound chicken to ¼-inch thickness. Place ham slice, cheese slice and ¼ cup spinach on each chicken piece and roll chicken from short end, jellyroll-style. Secure each roll with toothpick.

- Place carrots in sprayed slow cooker and top with chicken rolls. Heat soup with a little water in saucepan just to thin and pour over rolls. Cover and cook on LOW for 6 to 8 hours.

- Cook rice according to package directions and serve carrots, chicken rolls and sauce over rice. Serves 6.

*TIP: Squeeze spinach between paper towels to completely remove excess moisture.

Hot Shot Chicken

4 boneless, skinless chicken breast halves
4 green onions with tops, chopped
1 teaspoon dried rosemary
1 teaspoon dried sage
1 teaspoon dried thyme
3 cloves garlic, minced
1 (12 ounce) bottle or can beer

■ Preheat broiler.

■ Sprinkle salt and pepper generously over chicken. Place in sprayed baking dish and broil in oven to brown chicken on both sides or brown in skillet.

■ Place chicken in sprayed slow cooker and sprinkle with onions, rosemary, sage, thyme and garlic. Pour beer around chicken and cook on LOW for 4 hours. Serves 4.

Garlic is actually considered both a vegetable and an herb. Garlic has been used medicinally for thousands of years since ancient Greek and Roman times.

Colorful Chicken with Cashews

5 boneless, skinless chicken breast halves, cut
    into 1-inch strips
2 ribs celery, sliced
¼ cup soy sauce
¼ teaspoon ginger
½ cup chicken broth
1 (8 ounce) can sliced bamboo shoots, drained
½ cup Chinese pea pods
½ cup cashews, toasted
2 tablespoons cornstarch
Rice, cooked

- Place chicken strips and celery in sprayed slow cooker. Add soy sauce, ginger, broth and a little salt and pepper.

- Cover and cook on LOW for 4 to 4 hours 30 minutes.

- Increase heat to HIGH and add bamboo shoots, pea pods and cashews. Dissolve cornstarch in 2 tablespoons water in bowl and stir into slow cooker.

- Cover and cook for about 25 minutes or until thickened, stirring once. Serve over rice. Serves 6.

Never-Fail Chicken Spaghetti

6 boneless, skinless chicken breast halves, cooked, cubed
2 (10 ounce) cans cream of chicken soup
½ cup milk
1 (4 ounce) can sliced mushrooms, drained
¼ cup (½ stick) butter, melted
1 (12 ounce) package thin spaghetti
1 (5 ounce) package grated parmesan cheese

■ Combine chicken, soup, milk, mushrooms and butter in sprayed slow cooker; stir until blended well. Cover and cook on LOW for 6 to 8 hours.

■ Cook spaghetti according to package instructions and place on serving platter. Spoon chicken mixture and sauce over spaghetti and top with cheese. Serves 6 to 8.

According to the National Geographic, scientists have settled the old dispute about which came first - the chicken or the egg. They say that reptiles were laying eggs thousands of years before chickens appeared, and the first chicken came from an egg laid by a bird that was not quite a chicken. Clearly, the egg came first.

Stuff-it Chicken

5 boneless, skinless chicken breast halves
2 (10 ounce) cans cream of chicken soup
1 (6 ounce) box chicken stuffing mix
1 (16 ounce) package frozen green peas, thawed

■ Place chicken breasts in sprayed large slow cooker. Heat cream of chicken soup with a little water in a saucepan to thin. Pour over chicken.

■ Combine stuffing mix with ingredients on package directions in bowl and spoon over chicken and soup. Cover and cook on LOW for 5 to 6 hours.

■ Sprinkle drained green peas over top of stuffing. Cover and cook for additional 45 to 50 minutes. Serves 4 to 5.

TIP: For a nice variation, substitute 1 (10 ounce) can fiesta nacho cheese soup for 1 can of cream of chicken soup.

Mushroom Chicken

4 boneless, skinless chicken breasts halves
1 (15 ounce) can tomato sauce
2 (4 ounce) cans sliced mushrooms, drained
1 (10 ounce) package frozen chopped bell peppers
**   and onions**
2 teaspoons Italian seasoning
1 teaspoon minced garlic

- Brown chicken breasts in skillet and place in sprayed oval slow cooker.

- Combine tomato sauce, mushrooms, onions and peppers, Italian seasoning, garlic, and ¼ cup water in bowl and spoon over chicken breasts. Cover and cook on LOW for 4 to 5 hours. Serves 4.

Family meals teach basic manners and social skills that children need to be successful in life. What they learn will help them in new situations and give them more confidence because they will know how to act and what to say and do.

Chicken a la Orange

5 - 6 boneless, skinless chicken breast halves
1 - 2 tablespoons salt-free garlic and herb seasoning
2 (11 ounce) cans mandarin oranges, drained
1 (6 ounce) can frozen orange juice concentrate
1 tablespoon lemon juice
1 (10 ounce) can chicken broth
2 tablespoons cornstarch
2 - 3 cups cooked rice

- Place chicken breasts in sprayed slow cooker and sprinkle with garlic-herb seasoning.

- Combine oranges, orange juice concentrate, lemon juice, broth, cornstarch and ⅓ cup water in bowl, mix well. Pour mixture into slow cooker. Cover and cook on LOW for 6 to 8 hours.

- Place cooked rice on serving platter and top with chicken and sauce. Serves 5 to 6.

You can't trust a dog to guard your food.

Oregano Chicken

½ cup (1 stick) butter, melted
1 (1 ounce) packet Italian salad dressing
1 tablespoon lemon juice
4 - 5 boneless, skinless chicken breast halves
2 tablespoons dried oregano

- Combine butter, dressing and lemon juice in bowl and mix well.

- Place chicken breasts in sprayed large slow cooker. Spoon butter-lemon juice mixture over chicken. Cover and cook on LOW for 4 to 5 hours.

- Baste chicken with pan juices, sprinkle oregano over chicken and cook 1 additional hour. Serves 4 to 6.

TIP: *This recipe works well with boneless pork chops instead of chicken. For a complete meal, add a 10 ounce can French onion soup and serve over thin spaghetti.*

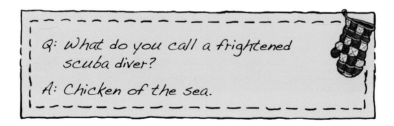

Q: What do you call a frightened scuba diver?

A: Chicken of the sea.

Chicken and Artichokes

¼ cup (½ stick) plus 2 tablespoons butter, divided
6 boneless, skinless chicken breast halves
1 (14 ounce) jar water-packed artichoke hearts, drained
1 (8 ounce) can sliced water chestnuts, drained
2 red bell peppers, seeded, cut into strips
1 (14 ounce) can chicken broth
1 (10 ounce) can cream of celery soup
1 (8 ounce) package shredded Italian cheese
1½ cups seasoned breadcrumbs

■ Melt ¼ cup butter in large skillet on medium heat, lightly
  brown chicken and place in sprayed slow cooker.

■ Cut each artichoke heart in half and place artichokes, water
  chestnuts and bell peppers around chicken.

■ Combine broth, celery soup and cheese in bowl, mix well
  and pour over chicken-artichoke mixture. Cover and cook
  on LOW for 7 to 9 hours.

■ Ten minutes before serving, place breadcrumbs and
  2 tablespoons melted butter in pan and stir until crumbs
  are well coated with butter. Heat in 325°F (165°C) oven for
  about 10 minutes. Sprinkle over dish. Serves 6.

Chicken and Pasta

1 onion, chopped
1 cup fresh mushroom halves
3 boneless, skinless chicken breast halves
1 (15 ounce) can Italian stewed tomatoes
1 teaspoon chicken bouillon granules
1 teaspoon minced garlic
1 teaspoon Italian seasoning
1 (8 ounce) package fettuccini
1 (4 ounce) package grated parmesan cheese

■ Place onion and mushrooms in sprayed slow cooker. Cut chicken into 1-inch pieces and place over vegetables.

■ Combine stewed tomatoes, chicken bouillon, garlic and Italian seasoning in small bowl. Pour over chicken. Cover and cook on LOW for 5 to 6 hours.

■ Cook fettuccini according to package directions and drain. Serve chicken over fettuccini and sprinkle with parmesan cheese. Serves 4.

TIP: Add ¼ cup butter for a richer taste.

Broccoli-Cheese Chicken

4 boneless, skinless chicken breast halves
2 tablespoons butter, melted
1 (10 ounce) can broccoli-cheese soup
¼ cup milk
1 (10 ounce) package frozen broccoli spears
Rice, cooked

- Dry chicken breasts with paper towels and place in sprayed oval slow cooker.

- Combine melted butter, soup and milk in bowl and spoon over chicken. Cover and cook on LOW for 4 to 6 hours.

- Place broccoli over chicken. Cover and cook for additional 1 hour. Serve over rice. Serves 4.

Removing the lid of a slow cooker will cause heat to escape. It will take approximately 20 minutes for the cooker to bring the heat back to the level it was before the lid was lifted.

Chicken Fajitas

2 pounds boneless, skinless chicken breast halves
1 onion, thinly sliced
1 red bell pepper, seeded, julienned
1 teaspoon ground cumin
1½ teaspoons chili powder
1 tablespoon lime juice
½ cup chicken broth
8 - 10 warm flour tortillas
Guacamole
Sour cream
Lettuce and tomatoes

- Cut chicken into diagonal strips and place in sprayed slow cooker. Top with onion and bell pepper.

- Combine cumin, chili powder, lime juice and chicken broth in bowl and pour over chicken and vegetables. Cover and cook on LOW for 5 to 7 hours.

- Serve several slices of chicken mixture with sauce into center of each warm tortilla and fold. Serve with guacamole, sour cream, lettuce and/or tomatoes or plain. Serves 4 to 6.

Picante Chicken

4 boneless, skinless chicken breast halves
1 green bell pepper, seeded, cut in rings
1 (16 ounce) jar picante sauce
⅓ cup packed brown sugar
1 tablespoon mustard

■ Place chicken breasts in sprayed slow cooker with bell pepper rings over top of chicken.

■ Combine picante, brown sugar and mustard in bowl and spoon over top of chicken. Cover and cook on LOW for 4 to 5 hours. Serves 4.

Chicken and Lima Bean Stew

1½ pound boneless, skinless chicken thighs, cubed
1 (28 ounce) can diced tomatoes
1 (15 ounce) can baby lima beans, drained
1 (15 ounce) can whole kernel corn, drained
1 tablespoon chopped garlic
1 tablespoon ground cumin
1 tablespoon dried oregano
3 tablespoons Worcestershire sauce
¼ cup tomato paste

■ Place all ingredients in sprayed slow cooker and mix well.
  Cover and cook on LOW 5 to 6 hours. Serves 6.

Since antiquity, garlic has been noted
for its special powers as a flavor
enhancement for foods and for its
suspected medicinal uses. Today it
may have a positive effect on lowering
cholesterol levels, reducing high blood
pressure and maybe even fighting off some
cancers.

Company Chicken Roll-Ups

6 boneless, skinless chicken breast halves
6 slices prosciutto
6 slices Mozzarella cheese
½ teaspoon dried sage
¾ cup chicken broth
2 ribs celery, thinly sliced
1 green bell pepper, seeded, chopped
3 tablespoons cornstarch
½ cup half-and-half cream
Rice, cooked

- Place chicken between 2 sheets of wax paper and pound with meat mallet to ½-inch thick.

- Place each slice of prosciutto on wax paper, top with chicken breast and slice of cheese. Sprinkle with sage and a little salt and pepper; roll jellyroll-style and secure with toothpicks. Place in sprayed slow cooker. Add chicken broth; cover and cook on LOW for 5 to 6 hours.

- Add celery and bell pepper. Dissolve cornstarch in half-and-half cream in bowl and stir into slow cooker. Increase heat to HIGH and cook for additional 20 minutes or until mixture has thickened. Serve over rice and top roll-ups with sauce. Serves 6.

Everybody's Favorite Dumplings

4 large boneless, skinless chicken breast halves
¼ cup (½ stick) butter, melted
2 (10 ounce) cans cream of chicken soup
1 small onion, finely chopped
2 ribs celery, sliced
2 (10 ounce) packages refrigerated biscuits

■ Place chicken breasts, butter, soup, onion and celery in sprayed large slow cooker. Fill with enough water to cover. Cover and cook on HIGH for 5 to 6 hours.

■ About 30 minutes before serving, remove chicken breasts with slotted spoon and cut chicken into small pieces, return to slow cooker. Tear each biscuit into several pieces and gradually drop pieces into slow cooker. Cook until dough is no longer raw in center.

■ Remove liner bowl from slow cooker and serve right from the bowl. Serves 8.

Easy Chicken Pie

1¼ pounds boneless, skinless chicken thighs
¼ cup finely chopped onion
1 (10 ounce) can chicken soup
1 cup milk, divided
2 ribs celery, thinly sliced
2¼ cups biscuit mix
1 (16 ounce) package frozen mixed vegetables, thawed

- Place chicken in sprayed slow cooker.

- Combine onion, soup, ⅓ cup milk and celery in small bowl, mix well. Spoon over chicken. Cover and cook on LOW for 8 to 10 hours.

- Prepare and bake 8 biscuits using biscuit mix and remaining milk as directed on package. While biscuits are baking, gently stir vegetables into chicken mixture. Increase heat to HIGH, cover and cook for additional 15 minutes.

- To serve, split each biscuit and place bottoms in individual soup bowls. Spoon about ¾ cup chicken mixture on top of biscuits and place tops of biscuits over chicken mixture. Serves 8.

Honey-Baked Chicken

2 small fryer chickens, quartered
Oil
½ cup (1 stick) butter, melted
⅔ cup honey
¼ cup dijon-style mustard
1 teaspoon curry powder

- Brown chicken over medium-hot heat in skillet with a
  little oil.

- Place chicken pieces in sprayed large slow cooker and
  sprinkle a little salt over chicken.

- Combine butter, honey, mustard and curry powder in bowl
  and mix well. Pour over chicken quarters. Cover and
  cook on LOW for 6 to 8 hours. Baste chicken once during
  cooking. Serves 6 to 8.

Turkey and Mushroom Soup

A great way to use leftover chicken or turkey

2 cups sliced shitake or sliced button mushrooms
2 ribs celery, sliced
1 small onion, chopped
2 tablespoons butter
1 (15 ounce) can sliced carrots
2 (14 ounce) cans chicken broth
½ cup orzo pasta
2 cups cooked, chopped turkey

■ Saute mushrooms, celery and onion in butter in skillet until onions are translucent.

■ Transfer vegetables to sprayed slow cooker and add carrots, broth, orzo and turkey. (Do not use smoked turkey.) Cover and cook on LOW for 2 to 3 hours or on HIGH for 1 to 2 hours. Serves 4 to 6.

TIP: Make a main dish by omitting 1 can chicken broth and adding 1 cup turkey. Place in a casserole dish and sprinkle with slivered almonds. Bake at 350°F (175°C) for about 10 to 15 minutes.

Corny Turkey Soup

1 onion, chopped
1 red bell pepper, seeded, chopped
1 (15 ounce) can cream-style corn
1 (15 ounce) can whole kernel corn
2 (14 ounce) cans chicken broth
1 cup whipping cream
2 - 3 cups cooked, cubed turkey
4 green onions, sliced

■ Combine onion, bell pepper, cream-style corn, whole kernel corn, broth, cream and cubed turkey in sprayed slow cooker.

■ Cover and cook on LOW for 5 to 7 hours. Scatter a few sliced green onions over each serving. Serves 4 to 6.

A group of chess players were checking into a hotel and talking to each other in the lobby about a tournament. After some time the hotel manager asked them to leave the lobby. "Why?" said a chess player.

"Because," replied the manager, "I don't like a bunch of chess nuts boasting in an open foyer."

Turkey and Rice Soup

**1 (10 ounce) package frozen chopped bell peppers and
onions, thawed**
¼ cup (½ stick) butter, melted
2 (14 ounce) cans turkey or chicken broth
1 (6 ounce) box roasted garlic long grain-wild rice mix
2 cups cooked, diced turkey
2 (10 ounce) cans cream of chicken soup
1 cup milk
1 (8 ounce) can green peas, drained

■ Combine bell peppers and onions, butter, turkey broth, rice
and turkey in sprayed slow cooker.

■ Heat cream of chicken soup and milk in saucepan over low
heat. Stir out lumps and pour over turkey.

■ Cover and cook on LOW for 6 to 8 hours. One hour before
serving, add peas. Serves 6.

In 1994 in a _Reader's Digest_ national
poll of high school seniors, Lou
Harris reported higher school
scores among seniors who ate with
their families. He also found that
high school seniors were happier with
themselves and prospects for the
future than seniors who did not eat at
home regularly.

Fresh Beefy Vegetable Soup

1 pound lean ground beef
1 onion, chopped
1 (15 ounce) can Italian stewed tomatoes
1 (8 ounce) can whole kernel corn
1 large potato, peeled, cubed
1 carrot, thinly sliced
2 (14 ounce) cans beef broth
2 tablespoons flour

■ Brown beef and onion in large, heavy soup pot over medium heat. Add stewed tomatoes, corn, potato, carrot, beef broth and 2 cups water. Bring to boil, reduce heat and simmer for 1 hour.

■ Combine flour and ¼ cup water in bowl and stir to make paste. On medium heat, add paste to soup with a little salt and pepper and cook, stirring constantly until soup thickens. Serves 6 to 8.

TIP: For an extra "kick", sprinkle hot sauce on top of individual bowls of soup.

This is a great recipe for leftovers. If you've got a leftover vegetable in the refrigerator, throw it in the pot!

Children who eat at home almost every night during the week are more likely to make better grades and perform better in school than those who do not.

Italian Beefy Veggie Soup

1 pound lean ground beef
2 (15 ounce) cans Italian stewed tomatoes
2 (14 ounce) cans beef broth
2 teaspoons Italian seasoning
1 (16 ounce) package frozen mixed vegetables
⅓ cup shell macaroni, optional
1 (8 ounce) package shredded Italian cheese

- Cook beef in large soup pot for 5 minutes. Stir in tomatoes, broth, 1 cup water, seasoning, mixed vegetables, macaroni and a little salt and pepper.

- Bring to boil, reduce heat and simmer for 10 to 15 minutes or until macaroni is tender.

- Ladle into individual serving bowls and sprinkle several tablespoons cheese over top of soup. Serves 8.

TIP: Great for leftover roast, flat-iron steak or pot roasts.

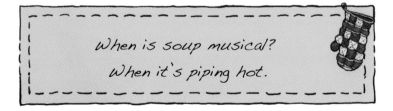

When is soup musical?
When it's piping hot.

Southwestern Round-Up

1½ pounds lean ground beef
2 (15 ounce) cans kidney beans with liquid
1 (15 ounce) can ranch-style (chili) beans, drained
2 (15 ounce) cans whole kernel corn with liquid
2 (15 ounce) cans Mexican stewed tomatoes
2 (1 ounce) packets taco seasoning

■ Brown beef in large soup pot, stir until beef crumbles and drain. Add beans, corn, tomatoes and 1½ cups water.

■ Bring to boil, reduce heat and stir in taco seasoning. Simmer for 25 minutes. Serves 8.

The Indians who lived in the New World and Mexico used chile peppers, beans, corn and squash in most of their dishes. These ingredients have developed into a regional cuisine that is known around the world.

Kitchen-Sink Taco Soup

1¼ pounds lean ground beef
1 onion, chopped
1 (.04 ounce) packet ranch dressing mix
2 (15 ounce) cans black beans with liquid
1 (15 ounce) can whole kernel corn with liquid
1 (15 ounce) can cream-style corn
3 (15 ounce) cans Mexican stewed tomatoes with liquid

- Brown ground beef and onion in skillet, drain and stir in ranch dressing mix.

- Combine beef-onion mixture, beans, corn, cream-style corn and stewed tomatoes in roasting pan.

- Bring to boil, lower heat and simmer for 10 to 15 minutes. Serves 6.

TIP: Serve over tortilla chips and sprinkle with cheese.

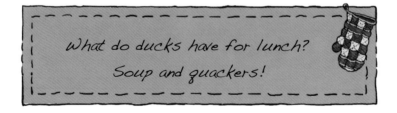

What do ducks have for lunch?
Soup and quackers!

Chunky Beefy Noodles

1 pound beef round steak, cubed
1 onion, chopped
2 ribs celery, sliced
1 tablespoon oil
1 tablespoon chili powder
1 (15 ounce) can stewed tomatoes
2 (14 ounce) cans beef broth
½ (8 ounce) package egg noodles
1 green bell pepper, seeded, chopped

- Cook and stir cubed steak, onion and celery in soup pot with oil for 15 minutes or until beef browns.

- Stir in 2 cups water, 1 teaspoon salt, chili powder, stewed tomatoes and beef broth.

- Bring to boil, reduce heat and simmer for 1 hour 30 minutes to 2 hours or until beef is tender.

- Stir in noodles and bell pepper and heat to boiling. Reduce heat and simmer for 10 to 15 minutes or until noodles are tender. Serves 6.

Meatball Supper

1 (18 ounce) package frozen, cooked Italian meatballs
2 (14 ounce) cans beef broth
2 (15 ounce) cans Italian stewed tomatoes
1 (16 ounce) package frozen stew vegetables

■ Place meatballs, beef broth and stewed tomatoes in large
  saucepan. Bring to boil, reduce heat and simmer for
  10 minutes or until meatballs are thoroughly hot.

■ Add vegetables and cook on medium heat for 10 minutes.
  Serves 6 to 8.

TIP: If you like your soup thicker, mix 2 tablespoons cornstarch
in ¼ cup water and stir into soup, bring to boiling and stir
constantly until soup thickens.

In southern Italy, soup is said to
relieve your hunger, quench your
thirst, fill your stomach, clean your
teeth, make you sleep, help you digest
and color your cheeks.

Sausage-Tortellini Soup

1 pound Italian sausage
1 onion, chopped
2 (14 ounce) cans beef broth
1 medium zucchini, halved, sliced
1 (15 ounce) can Italian stewed tomatoes
1 (9 ounce) package refrigerated meat-filled tortellini
Mozzarella cheese

- Cook and stir sausage and onion in soup pot on medium heat until sausage is light brown.

- Drain and stir in beef broth, 1½ cups water, zucchini, tomatoes, tortellini and a little salt and pepper.

- Bring to a boil, reduce heat and simmer for 20 minutes or until tortellini are tender.

- Ladle into individual soup bowls and sprinkle each serving with cheese. Serves 6.

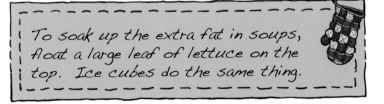

To soak up the extra fat in soups, float a large leaf of lettuce on the top. Ice cubes do the same thing.

Black Bean Barbecue Fix

1 onion, finely chopped
2 tablespoons olive oil
2 teaspoons minced garlic
2 (14 ounce) cans chicken broth
3 (15 ounce) cans black beans, rinsed, drained
1 (10 ounce) can diced tomatoes and green chilies
1 pound shredded barbecue beef
2 tablespoons red wine vinegar
Shredded Monterey Jack cheese

- Saute onion in oil in soup pot over medium heat, stir in garlic and saute 1 more minute.

- Stir in broth, beans and tomatoes and green chilies. Reduce heat, simmer for 15 minutes and stir often.

- Process 1 cup bean mixture in food processor until smooth. Return puree to soup pot, add beef and simmer for 10 minutes.

- Stir in vinegar and garnish each bowl with cheese. Serves 6 to 8.

Blue Ribbon Beef Stew

1 (2½ pound) boneless beef chuck roast, cubed
⅓ cup flour
2 (14 ounce) cans beef broth
1 teaspoon dried thyme
2 teaspoons minced garlic
1 pound new (red) potatoes with peel, sliced
2 large carrots, sliced
3 ribs celery, sliced
2 onions, finely chopped
1 (4.5 ounce) can green peas, drained

■ Dredge beef in flour and 1 teaspoon salt; set aside leftover
   flour. Brown half beef in stew pot over medium heat for
   about 10 minutes and transfer to plate.

■ Repeat with remaining beef. Add set aside flour to stew pot
   and cook, stirring constantly, for 1 minute.

■ Stir in beef broth, ½ cup water, thyme and garlic and
   bring to a boil Reduce heat, simmer for 50 minutes and
   stir occasionally.

■ Add potatoes, carrots, celery and onion and cook for
   30 minutes. Stir in peas and a little salt and pepper;
   heat to boiling. Serve hot. Serves 6.

Down Home Meat and Potato Stew

2 pounds beef stew meat
2 (15 ounce) cans new potatoes, drained
1 (15 ounce) can sliced carrots, drained
1 onion, chopped
2 (10 ounce) cans French onion soup

- Season meat with a little salt and pepper and cook with 2 cups water in large pot for 1 hour. Add potatoes, carrots, onion and onion soup and mix well.

- Bring to boil, reduce heat and simmer for 30 minutes. Serves 6.

We may live without poetry, music
    and art;
We may live without conscience, and
    live without heart;
We may live without friends, we may
    live without books;
But civilized man cannot live without
    cooks.
                —Owen Meredith

Blue Norther Winner

*When a cold front moves into the south,
it's called a "blue norther". This is a great
choice for one of those cold, winter days.*

1½ pounds lean ground beef
1 (1 ounce) packet taco seasoning
1 (.04 ounce) packet ranch dressing mix
1 (15 ounce) can whole kernel corn, drained
1 (15 ounce) can kidney beans with liquid
2 (15 ounce) cans pinto beans
2 (15 ounce) cans Mexican stewed tomatoes
1 (10 ounce) can diced tomatoes and green chilies

■ Brown ground beef in large roasting pan. Add both packets
  seasonings and mix well.

■ Add corn, beans, stewed tomatoes, tomatoes and green
  chilies, and 1 cup water; mix well and simmer for about
  30 minutes. Serves 8.

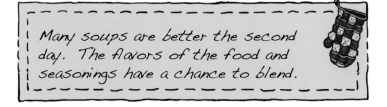

*Many soups are better the second
day. The flavors of the food and
seasonings have a chance to blend.*

Stroganoff Stew

1 (1 ounce) packet onion soup mix
2 (10 ounce) cans golden mushroom soup
2 pounds stew meat
1 (8 ounce) carton sour cream
Noodles, cooked

- Preheat oven to 275°F (135°C).

- Combine soup mix, mushroom soup and 2 soup cans water and pour over stew meat in roasting pan.

- Cover tightly and bake for 6 to 8 hours.

- When ready to serve, stir in sour cream, return mixture to oven until it heats thoroughly and serve over noodles. Serves 6.

If you need to add water to stew, use room temperature water and not boiling water because it may toughen meat.

Polish-Vegetable Stew

Olive oil
1 onion, sliced
2 carrots, peeled, sliced
2 (15 ounce) cans stewed tomatoes
2 (15 ounce) cans new potatoes, drained, quartered
1 pound Polish sausage, sliced
1 (9 ounce) package coleslaw mix

■ Place a little oil in large stew pot. Cook onion and carrots for 3 minutes or until tender-crisp. Add tomatoes and ½ cup water; stir well.

■ Stir potatoes and sausage in soup mixture. Bring to boil, reduce heat and simmer for 10 minutes.

■ Stir in coleslaw mix and cook on medium heat for additional 8 minutes, stirring occasionally. Serves 6.

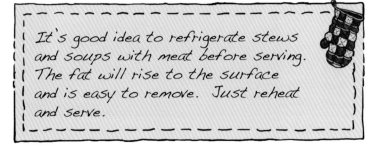

It's good idea to refrigerate stews and soups with meat before serving. The fat will rise to the surface and is easy to remove. Just reheat and serve.

Deer Camp Venison Chili

2 onions, chopped
2½ pounds ground venison
1 (15 ounce) can Mexican stewed tomatoes
½ (15 ounce) can beef broth
¾ cup red wine
2 teaspoons minced garlic
3 tablespoons chili powder
1 teaspoon ground cumin

■ Cook onions over medium-high heat until translucent. Add venison and brown until meat crumbles; stir often.

■ Stir in beef broth, tomatoes, wine, garlic, chili powder, cumin and a little salt. Bring to boil, reduce heat and simmer for 1 hour, stirring occasionally. Remove salt pork before serving. Serves 6.

Herbs will have a more intense flavor if they are added when the soup is almost ready to serve.

Corned Beef Supper

2 - 3 pounds corned eye of round beef
9 peppercorns
¼ cup red wine vinegar
1 (12 ounce) package baby carrots
6 medium potatoes, peeled, halved
1 medium head cabbage, coarsely sliced in 6 wedges

■ Place beef, peppercorns, vinegar and 7 cups water in
  sprayed slow cooker. Arrange carrots and potatoes around
  beef. Cover and cook on LOW for 8 to 10 hours.

■ Place cabbage wedges around sides of slow cooker and
  cook for additional 15 to 20 minutes. Discard liquid in slow
  cooker. Serves 6.

TIP: In order to keep cabbage pieces together during cooking,
   leave a bit of the core with each wedge.

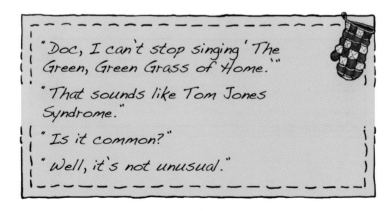

"Doc, I can't stop singing 'The
Green, Green Grass of Home.'"

"That sounds like Tom Jones
Syndrome."

"Is it common?"

"Well, it's not unusual."

Herb-Crusted Beef Roast

1 (2 - 3 pound) beef rump roast
¼ cup chopped fresh parsley
¼ cup chopped fresh oregano leaves
½ teaspoon dried rosemary leaves
1 teaspoon minced garlic
1 tablespoon oil
6 slices thick-cut bacon

■ Rub roast with a little salt and pepper. Combine parsley, oregano, rosemary, garlic and oil in small bowl and press mixture on top and sides of roast.

■ Place roast in sprayed slow cooker. Place bacon over top of beef and tuck ends under. Cover and cook on LOW for 6 to 8 hours. Serves 4 to 6.

Slow cookers aren't just for cooking when it's cold and wintry outside. It's also great to use in the summer so you don't heat up the kitchen from the oven and you use much less energy with the slow cooker than the oven.

Sweet and Spicy Brisket

½ cup packed brown sugar
1 tablespoon Cajun seasoning
2 teaspoons lemon pepper
1 tablespoon Worcestershire sauce
1 (3 - 4 pound) trimmed beef brisket

■ Combine brown sugar, Cajun seasoning, lemon pepper and Worcestershire in small bowl and spread over brisket.

■ Place brisket in sprayed oval slow cooker. Cover and cook on LOW for 6 to 8 hours. Serves 6 to 8.

Meat is usually the focal point of a meal. It can take a big bite out of the food budget. Less expensive cuts of meat can be just as delicious as pricier ones. The secret is the method of cooking - long and slow. The slow cooker is an exceptionally useful device for creating really tender and tasty meat dishes.

Smoked Brisket

1 (4 - 6 pound) trimmed brisket
1 (4 ounce) bottle liquid smoke
Garlic salt
Celery salt
Worcestershire sauce
1 onion, chopped
1 (6 ounce) bottle barbecue sauce

- Place brisket in large shallow dish and pour liquid smoke over top. Sprinkle with garlic salt and celery salt. Cover and refrigerate overnight.

- Before cooking, drain liquid smoke and douse brisket with Worcestershire sauce. Place chopped onion in slow cooker and place brisket on top of onion. Cover and cook on LOW for 6 to 8 hours.

- Pour barbecue sauce over brisket and cook for additional 1 hour. Serves 6 to 8.

Tougher or cheaper cuts of meat cook better on LOW in the slow cooker and have a better chance of becoming tender with longer cooking times.

Favorite Pot Roast and Veggies

1 (2 pound) chuck roast
4 - 5 medium potatoes, peeled, quartered
4 large carrots, quartered
1 onion, quartered
1 (14 ounce) can beef broth, divided
2 tablespoons cornstarch

- Trim fat from pieces of roast. Cut roast into 2 equal pieces. Brown pieces of roast in skillet. (Coat pieces with flour, salt and pepper if you'd like a little "breading" on the outside.)

- Place potatoes, carrots and onion in sprayed slow cooker and mix well. Place browned beef over vegetables. Pour 1½ cups broth over beef and vegetables. Set aside remaining broth and refrigerate.

- Cover and cook on LOW for 8 to 9 hours. About 5 minutes before serving, remove beef and vegetables with slotted spoon and place on serving platter. Cover to keep warm.

- Pour liquid from slow cooker into medium saucepan. Blend remaining ½ cup broth and cornstarch in bowl until smooth and add to liquid in saucepan. Boil for 1 minute and stir constantly to thicken for gravy.

- Serve gravy with roast and veggies; season with a little salt and pepper, if desired. Serves 4 to 6.

Justice with Short Ribs

Flour for coating ribs
3 pounds beef short ribs
3 tablespoons olive oil
1 onion, thinly sliced
½ cup chili sauce
¼ cup packed brown sugar
3 tablespoons vinegar
2 tablespoons flour

■ Coat ribs with lots of salt and pepper; then dredge in flour, coating well. Brown short ribs in oil in large skillet on medium-high heat until light brown.

■ Place onion, chili sauce, brown sugar and vinegar in sprayed slow cooker; mix thoroughly. Add browned ribs. Cover and cook on LOW for 6 to 8 hours.

■ Remove ribs to serving platter and turn slow cooker to HIGH heat. Combine 2 tablespoons flour with ½ cup water in bowl and stir into sauce in slow cooker. Cook for 10 minutes or until mixture thickens. Spoon sauce over ribs. Serves 6.

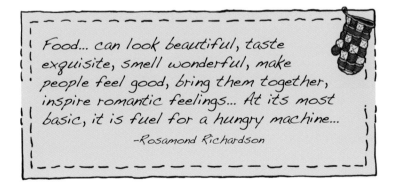

Food... can look beautiful, taste exquisite, smell wonderful, make people feel good, bring them together, inspire romantic feelings... At its most basic, it is fuel for a hungry machine...

—Rosamond Richardson

Mushroom Round Steak

1½ - 2 pounds round steak
1 (1 ounce) packet onion soup mix
½ cup dry red wine
1 (8 ounce) carton fresh mushrooms, sliced
1 (10 ounce) can French onion soup

■ Cut round steak in serving-size pieces and place in sprayed oval slow cooker.

■ Combine soup mix, red wine, mushrooms, French onion soup and ½ cup water in bowl. Spoon over steak pieces.

■ Cover and cook on LOW for 7 to 8 hours. Serves 4 to 6.

Slow cooking retains most of the moisture in food, so if a recipe has too much liquid at the end of cooking time, remove cover, increase heat to HIGH and cook for another 45 minutes to reduce the liquid.

Pasta with Seasoned Beef Tips

2 - 2½ pounds lean beef stew meat
2 cups frozen, small whole onions, thawed
1 green bell pepper, seeded
1 (6 ounce) jar pitted Greek olives or ripe olives
½ cup sun-dried tomatoes in oil, drained, chopped
1 (28 ounce) jar marinara sauce
1 (8 ounce) package pasta twirls, cooked

■ Place beef and onions in sprayed slow cooker. Cut bell pepper in 1-inch cubes and add to slow cooker.

■ Add olives and tomatoes and pour marinara sauce over top. Cover and cook on LOW for 8 to 10 hours. Serve over pasta twirls. Serves 4 to 6.

"The price of freedom is eternal vigilance."

Thomas Jefferson

Round Steak Stroganoff

2 pounds beef round steak
¾ cup flour, divided
½ teaspoon mustard
2 onions, thinly sliced
½ pound fresh mushrooms, sliced
1 (10 ounce) can beef broth
¼ cup dry white wine or cooking wine
1 (8 ounce) carton sour cream
Rice or noodles, cooked

■ Trim excess fat from steak and cut into 3-inch strips about ½-inch wide.

■ Combine ½ cup flour, mustard and a little salt and pepper in bowl and toss with steak strips. Place strips in sprayed, oval slow cooker.

■ Cover with onions and mushrooms. Add beef broth and wine. Cover and cook on LOW for 8 to 10 hours.

■ Just before serving, combine sour cream and ¼ cup flour in bowl. Stir into cooker and cook for additional 10 to 15 minutes or until stroganoff thickens slightly. Serve over cooked rice or noodles. Serves 4 to 6.

Beef Roulades

1½ pounds beef flank steak
5 slices bacon
¾ cup finely chopped onion
1 (4 ounce) can mushrooms pieces
1 tablespoon Worcestershire sauce
⅓ cup Italian-seasoned breadcrumbs
1 (12 ounce) jar beef gravy
Mashed potatoes

■ Cut steak into 4 to 6 serving-size pieces. Cut bacon into small pieces and combine with onion, mushrooms, Worcestershire and breadcrumbs in bowl.

■ Place about ½ cup onion mixture on each piece of steak. Roll meat and secure ends with toothpicks. Dry beef rolls with paper towels. In skillet, brown steak rolls and transfer to sprayed slow cooker.

■ Pour gravy evenly over steaks to thoroughly moisten. Cover and cook on LOW for 7 to 9 hours. Serve with mashed potatoes. Serves 4 to 6.

TIP: *This is really good served with mashed potatoes. Have you tried instant mashed potatoes as a time-saver?*

Teriyaki Steak

1½ - 2 pounds flank steak
1 (15 ounce) can sliced pineapple with juice
1 tablespoon marinade for chicken
⅓ cup packed brown sugar
3 tablespoons soy sauce
½ teaspoon ground ginger
1 (14 ounce) can chicken broth
1 cup long grain rice

■ Roll flank steak, tie in place and cut into 7 to 8 individual
steaks.

■ Combine ½ cup pineapple juice, marinade for chicken,
brown sugar, soy sauce and ginger in bowl large enough for
marinade to cover individual steaks. Add steak rolls and
marinate for 1 hour in sauce. Discard marinade.

■ Pour chicken broth into sprayed slow cooker. Add rice and
¾ cup water. Place steaks over rice and broth. Cover and
cook on LOW for 8 to 10 hours. Serves 4 to 6.

*The most indispensable ingredient
of all good home cooking: love, for
those you are cooking for.*
　　　　　　　　　　–Sophia Loren

Crowd-Pleasing Pepper Steak

¼ cup flour
1½ pounds beef round steak
2 tablespoons canola oil
1 onion, chopped
2 large green bell peppers, seeded, julienned, divided
1 (15 ounce) can Italian stewed tomatoes
½ cup beef broth
1 tablespoon Worcestershire sauce
1 cup instant rice

■ Combine flour, 1 teaspoon each of salt and pepper in shallow bowl. Cut steak into strips and toss with flour mixture to coat thoroughly. Heat oil in skillet and cook steak strips until slightly brown; turn often.

■ Place steak, onion, 1 julienned bell pepper, tomatoes, broth and Worcestershire in sprayed slow cooker. Cover and cook on LOW for 7 to 9 hours.

■ Add remaining julienned pepper to slow cooker, cover and cook for 1 additional hour.

■ Cook rice according to package directions, place on serving platter and top with pepper steak. Serves 4.

Spectacular Beef and Broccoli

1 - 1½ pounds boneless round steak, cut into 1-inch cubes
1 (10 ounce) package frozen chopped bell peppers and
**   onions, thawed**
2 ribs celery, cut in 1-inch slices
1 (10 ounce) can beef broth
3 tablespoons teriyaki baste-and-glaze
2 tablespoons cornstarch
1 (16 ounce) package frozen broccoli florets, thawed
Rice, cooked

■ Place steak cubes, bell peppers and onions, celery, broth, teriyaki baste-and-glaze and ½ teaspoon pepper in sprayed slow cooker. Cover and cook on LOW for 8 to 10 hours.

■ Mix cornstarch with 2 to 3 tablespoons water in small bowl. Stir cornstarch mixture and broccoli florets into slow cooker, cover and cook for additional 25 to 30 minutes. Serve over rice. Serves 4 to 6.

When purchasing ground beef, remember that fat greatly contributes to its flavor. The lower the fat content, the drier it will be once cooked.

Italian Tortellini

½ **pound ground round steak**
1 **(1 pound) package bulk Italian sausage**
1 **(15 ounce) carton refrigerated marinara sauce**
1 **(15 ounce) can Italian stewed tomatoes with liquid**
1½ **cups sliced fresh mushrooms**
1 **(9 ounce) package refrigerated cheese tortellini**
1½ **cups shredded mozzarella cheese**

- Brown and cook ground beef and sausage in large skillet for about 10 minutes on medium-low heat and drain.

- Combine meat mixture, marinara sauce, tomatoes and mushrooms in sprayed slow cooker. Cover and cook on LOW 6 to 8 hours.

- Stir in tortellini and sprinkle with mozzarella cheese. Turn cooker to HIGH, cover and cook for additional 10 to 15 minutes or until tortellini is tender. Serves 4 to 6.

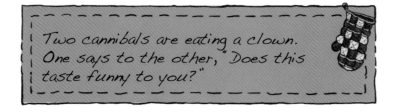

Two cannibals are eating a clown.
One says to the other, "Does this
taste funny to you?"

Select Beef-Potato Soup

2 (14 ounce) cans beef broth
1 (10 ounce) can cream of celery soup
1 cup half-and-half cream
1 pound boneless beef chuck, cut into 1-inch pieces
1 (5 ounce) box au gratin potato mix
½ teaspoon dried thyme
1 (15 ounce) can green peas, drained
Grated parmesan cheese

■ Pour beef broth and cream of celery soup into slow cooker
and whisk well. Place beef pieces, potato mix, thyme,
2 cups water in sprayed slow cooker.

■ over and cook on LOW for 7 to 8 hours or on HIGH for
3 hours 30 minutes to 4 hours.

■ (If cooking on HIGH, reduce heat to LOW.) Stir in half-and-
half cream and peas; cover and cook for additional 15 to
20 minutes. Sprinkle parmesan cheese over each serving.
Serves 4 to 5.

Two antennas met on a roof, fell in
love and got married. The ceremony
wasn't much, but the reception
was excellent.

Meat Loaf Magic

1½ pounds lean ground beef
⅔ cup cracker crumbs
2 eggs, beaten
2 tablespoons plus ½ cup ketchup, divided
¼ cup finely minced onion
¼ cup packed brown sugar
1 teaspoon mustard
½ teaspoon ground nutmeg

■ Make foil handles for meat loaf by cutting 3 (3 x 18-inch) strips of heavy foil. Place in bottom of slow cooker in crisscross strips and fold ends over top.

■ Combine beef, cracker crumbs, eggs, 2 tablespoons ketchup, onion, and about 1 teaspoon each of salt and pepper in large bowl. Shape into loaf and place in sprayed slow cooker. Fold ends of foil strips over loaf. Cover and cook on LOW for 5 to 6 hours.

■ A few minutes before serving, combine remaining ketchup, brown sugar, mustard and nutmeg in bowl and spoon over meatloaf. Cover and cook on HIGH for about 15 additional minutes. Lift meat loaf out with foil handles. Serves 6.

Cheeseburger Pie Supper

1 (5 ounce) box bacon and cheddar scalloped potatoes
⅓ cup milk
¼ cup (½ stick) butter, melted
1½ pounds lean ground beef
1 onion, coarsely chopped
Canola oil
1 (15 ounce) can whole kernel corn with liquid
1 (8 ounce) package shredded cheddar cheese

■ Place scalloped potatoes in sprayed slow cooker. Pour
  2¼ cups boiling water, milk and butter over potatoes.

■ Brown ground beef and onion in little oil in skillet, drain and
  spoon over potatoes. Top with corn. Cover and cook on
  LOW for 6 to 7 hours.

■ When ready to serve, sprinkle cheese over top.
  Serves 4 to 6.

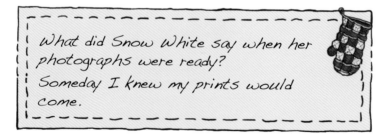

*What did Snow White say when her
photographs were ready?*
*Someday I knew my prints would
come.*

Pop's Beef-Potato Supper

2 pounds lean ground beef
1 (10 ounce) package frozen, chopped bell peppers and onions, thawed
3 ribs celery, sliced
1 (18 ounce) package frozen tater tots, thawed
1 (8 ounce) package shredded Velveeta® cheese
2 (10 ounce) cans cream of mushroom soup
1 soup can milk
1 (8 ounce) package shredded cheddar cheese

■ Cook ground beef in skillet over medium-high heat for about 10 minutes or until beef is no longer pink; stir often. Drain and place in sprayed slow cooker.

■ Combine bell peppers and onions, celery, tater tots and Velveeta® cheese in bowl. Heat soup and milk in saucepan just enough to thin soup. Pour over vegetables and stir well.

■ Cover and cook on LOW for 6 to 8 hours. Sprinkle with cheese. Serves 8 to 10.

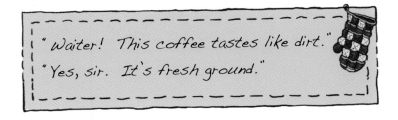

"Waiter! This coffee tastes like dirt."
"Yes, sir. It's fresh ground."

Amigos Taco Soup Olé

1½ **pounds lean ground beef**
2 **(15 ounce) cans chili beans with liquid**
1 **(15 ounce) can whole kernel corn with liquid**
2 **(15 ounce) cans stewed tomatoes**
1 **(10 ounce) can diced tomatoes and green chilies**
1 **(.04 ounce) packet ranch dressing mix**
1 **(1 ounce) packet taco seasoning**
Shredded cheddar cheese

■ Brown ground beef in large skillet, drain and transfer to sprayed slow cooker.

■ Add remaining ingredients and stir well. Cover and cook on LOW for 8 to 10 hours. When serving, sprinkle cheese over each serving. Serve 6 to 8.

> You can thicken soups by adding quick-cooking oats, a grated potato or mashing some of the vegetables.

Beef and Black Bean Soup

1 pound lean ground beef
2 onions, chopped
2 cups sliced celery
2 (14 ounce) cans beef broth
1 (15 ounce) can Mexican stewed tomatoes
2 (15 ounce) cans black beans, rinsed, drained

- Brown beef in skillet until no longer pink. Place in sprayed slow cooker.

- Add onions, celery, broth, tomatoes, black beans, ¾ cup water plus a little salt and pepper. Cover and cook on LOW for 6 to 7 hours or on HIGH for 3 hours to 3 hours 30 minutes. Serves 6 to 8.

TIP: If you like a zestier soup, add 1 teaspoon chili powder.

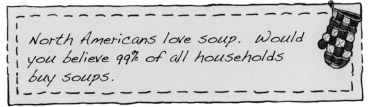

North Americans love soup. Would you believe 99% of all households buy soups.

Hearty Italian Vegetable Soup

1 pound lean ground beef
2 teaspoons minced garlic
1 green bell pepper, seeded, chopped
3 (14 ounce) cans beef broth
1 (15 ounce) can stewed tomatoes
2 (15 ounce) can cannellini beans, rinsed, drained
1 teaspoon Italian seasoning
2 medium zucchini, sliced
1 (10 ounce) package frozen chopped spinach, thawed

- Brown ground beef in skillet, drain and combine with garlic, bell pepper, broth, tomatoes, beans and Italian seasoning in sprayed slow cooker. Cover and cook on LOW for 5 to 7 hours.

- Stir in zucchini and chopped spinach and cook for additional 1 hour. Serves 6 to 8.

TIP: If you have pasta in the pantry, add it to the pot. You can put just about anything in this soup.

Beef and Barley Soup

1 pound lean ground beef
3 (14 ounce) cans beef broth
¾ cup quick-cooking barley
3 cups sliced carrots
2 cups sliced celery
2 teaspoons beef seasoning

■ Brown ground beef in skillet, drain and transfer to sprayed slow cooker.

■ Add beef broth, barley, carrots, celery and beef seasoning. Cover and cook on LOW for 7 to 8 hours. Serves 4.

Beefy Rice Soup

1 pound lean beef stew meat
1 (14 ounce) can beef broth
1 (7 ounce) box beef-flavored rice and vermicelli mix
1 (10 ounce) package frozen peas and carrots
2½ cups vegetable juice

■ Sprinkle stew meat with seasoned pepper, brown in non-stick skillet, drain and place in sprayed, large slow cooker.

■ Add broth, rice and vermicelli mix, peas and carrots, vegetable juice and 2 cups water. Cover and cook on LOW for 6 to 7 hours. Serves 4 to 6.

Green Chile-Beef Bake

1½ pounds lean ground beef
1 (10 ounce) package frozen chopped bell peppers and
    onions, thawed
1 (1 ounce) packet taco seasoning mix
2 (7 ounce) cans whole green chilies
1 (15 ounce) can refried beans
1 (16 ounce) jar thick-and-chunky salsa
8 - 10 cups slightly crushed tortilla chips
1 (12 ounce) package shredded Mexican 4-cheese blend

■ Brown beef in skillet and drain. Add bell peppers and
  onions and cook over medium heat for about 10 minutes.
  Stir in taco seasoning and ¼ cup water.

■ Cut chilies in half, remove seeds and arrange evenly in
  sprayed slow cooker. Add beef mixture and add refried
  beans evenly over beef. Top with remaining chilies. Pour
  salsa over all top. Do not stir. Cover and cook on LOW for
  8 to 10 hours.

■ Place about ¾ cup crushed tortilla chips on individual plates,
  spoon beef mixture over chips and top with about ¼ cup
  cheese. Serves 8 to 10.

Colorful Stuffed Peppers

6 medium red or green bell peppers, stemmed, seeded
1 pound lean ground beef
½ cup finely chopped onion
¾ cup instant rice
1 (15 ounce) can black beans, rinsed, drained
⅓ cup seasoned breadcrumbs
1 (8 ounce) package shredded Monterey Jack
   cheese, divided
1 (16 ounce) jar hot chunky salsa, divided

- Cook and brown ground beef in large skillet and stir to crumble. Drain, stir in onion, rice, beans, breadcrumbs, half cheese and half salsa and mix well. Spoon filling into bell peppers and place tops on each.

- Place ¾ cup water and remaining salsa in sprayed slow cooker. Arrange stuffed peppers around sides of cooker.

- Cover and cook on LOW for 6 to 7 hours or on HIGH for 3 hours to 3 hours 30 minutes.

- Transfer stuffed peppers to serving plate and sprinkle remaining cheese over tops. Serves 6.

TIP: These peppers can be served over hot cooked rice with sauce from slow cooker poured over the rice.

Slow Cooker Ziti

1 pound ground beef
1 tablespoon Italian seasoning
2 (26 ounce) cans spaghetti sauce
2 (8 ounce) packages shredded mozzarella cheese, divided
1 (15 ounce) carton ricotta cheese
1 cup grated parmesan cheese
1 (16 ounce) box ziti pasta

■ Brown ground beef in skillet and drain. Add Italian seasoning, sauce and 1 teaspoon each salt and pepper to meat.

■ Combine 1 package mozzarella, ricotta and parmesan in separate bowl.

■ In slow cooker, layer 2 cups meat mixture, half ziti and half cheese mixture. Repeat. Cover with remaining meat mixture. Cover and cook on LOW for 5 to 6 hours.

■ Top with remaining mozzarella and serve when cheese melts. Serves 6 to 8.

Knockout Minestrone

1 (15 ounce) can cannellini beans, rinsed, drained
1 (15 ounce) can pinto beans, drained
1 (15 ounce) can kidney beans, rinsed, drained
2 (15 ounce) cans Italian stewed tomatoes with liquid
1 pound boneless beef chuck, cut in ½-inch pieces
1 cup peeled, shredded carrots
1 cup dried favorite pasta
1 medium zucchini, sliced
Parmesan cheese

■ Combine beans, stewed tomatoes, beef, carrots and a
  little salt and pepper in sprayed slow cooker. Cover and
  cook on LOW for 8 to 9 hours or on HIGH for 4 hours to
  4 hours 30 minutes.

■ Add pasta and zucchini and cook on HIGH heat for 30 to
  45 minutes. Sprinkle each serving with a little parmesan
  cheese. Serves 8.

Minestrone soup comes from the
Italian word "minestra," which means
minister. Clergy ministered to the
poor by providing bowls of broth with
hearty vegetables.

South-of-the-Border Beef Stew

1½ - 2 pounds boneless, beef chuck roast
1 green bell pepper, seeded
2 onions, coarsely chopped
2 (15 ounce) cans pinto beans with liquid
½ cup rice
1 (14 ounce) can beef broth
2 (15 ounce) cans Mexican stewed tomatoes
1 cup mild or medium green salsa
2 teaspoons ground cumin
Flour tortillas

■ Trim beef and cut into 1-inch cubes. Brown beef in large skillet and transfer to sprayed large slow cooker.

■ Cut bell pepper into ½-inch slices. Add remaining ingredients with a little salt and 1½ cups water.

■ Cover and cook on LOW for 7 to 8 hours. Serve with warm flour tortillas. Serves 8.

Small portions of leftover soup can be frozen and added to new soups later on.

Fast Comfort Stew

1½ pounds premium beef stew meat
Oil
2 (10 ounce) cans French onion soup
1 (10 ounce) can cream of onion soup
1 (10 ounce) can cream of celery soup
1 (16 ounce) package frozen stew vegetables, thawed

- Brown meat in skillet with a little oil over medium-high heat. Place meat in sprayed slow cooker.

- Combine all soups and mix well. Spread evenly over meat, but do not stir.

- Turn slow cooker to HIGH and cook just long enough for ingredients to get hot, about 15 minutes.

- Change heat setting to LOW, cover and cook for 7 hours. Add vegetables and cook for additional 1 hour. Serves 6 to 8.

Browning meats reduces the fat content and improves the look of meats cooked in slow cookers.

Black Bean Stew Supper

1 pound pork sausage link, thinly sliced
2 onions, chopped
3 ribs celery, sliced
Olive oil
3 (15 ounce) cans black beans, drained, rinsed
2 (10 ounce) cans diced tomatoes and green chilies
2 (14 ounce) cans chicken broth

- Place sausage slices, onion and celery in stew pot with a little oil, cook until sausage is light brown and onion is soft and drain. Add beans, tomatoes and green chilies and broth.

- Bring to boil, reduce heat and simmer for 30 minutes. Take out about 2 cups stew mixture, pour into food processor and pulse until almost smooth.

- Return mixture to pot and stir to thicken stew. Return heat to high until stew is thoroughly hot. Serves 6.

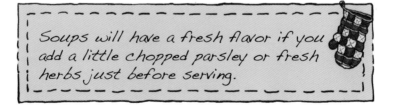

Soups will have a fresh flavor if you add a little chopped parsley or fresh herbs just before serving.

Tomato and White Bean Soup

2 tablespoons olive oil
1 onion, chopped
1 green bell pepper, seeded, chopped
1 (15 ounce) can diced tomatoes
2 (14 ounce) cans chicken broth
2 (15 ounce) cans navy beans, rinsed, drained
1½ cups cooked, cubed ham
½ cup chopped fresh parsley

- Combine olive oil, onion, bell pepper in large saucepan and saute for 5 minutes and stir constantly.

- Stir in tomatoes, broth, navy beans and ham and bring to boil. Reduce heat and simmer for 10 minutes.

- Pour into individual soup bowls and sprinkle parsley on top. Serves 4.

If your sauce, soup or stew is too salty, add a peeled potato to the pot and it will absorb the extra salt.

Good Ol' Bean Soup

3 tablespoons olive oil
1 cup shredded carrots
1 (16 ounce) package frozen chopped bell peppers
    and onions
2 (14 ounce) cans chicken broth
2 (15 ounce) cans pinto beans with jalapenos with liquid
2 cups cooked, diced ham

- Combine oil, carrots, and bell peppers and onions in soup
  pot and cook for 10 minutes.

- Add broth, pinto beans, ham and ½ cup water. Bring to
  boil, reduce heat and simmer for 15 minutes. Serves 6.

In ancient Greece, soup made of
peas, lentils and beans was sold in
stalls on the street as perhaps the
world's first fast food.

Hearty Bean and Ham Fare

What a great supper for a cold winter night!

1 (15 ounce) can sliced carrots, drained
1 cup chopped celery
¼ cup (½ stick) butter
2 - 3 cups cooked, diced ham
2 (15 ounce) cans navy beans with liquid
2 (15 ounce) cans jalapeno pinto beans with liquid
2 (14 ounce) cans chicken broth
2 teaspoons chili powder

■ Cook carrots and celery in soup pot with butter for about 8 minutes until tender-crisp.

■ Add diced ham, navy beans, pinto beans, chicken broth, chili powder and a little salt and pepper. Bring to boil and stir constantly for 3 minutes. Reduce heat and simmer for 15 minutes. Serves 8.

TIP: Cornbread is great with this soup.

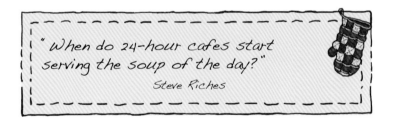

" When do 24-hour cafes start serving the soup of the day?"

Steve Riches

Ham and Black Bean Soup

2 cups dried black beans
1 cup cooked, diced ham
1 onion, chopped
1 carrot, chopped
2 (14 ounce) cans chicken broth
1 tablespoon ground cumin
2 tablespoons fresh cilantro
1 tablespoon chili powder
1 (8 ounce) carton sour cream

■ Wash beans, soak overnight and drain. Except for sour cream, place all ingredients and 1 teaspoon salt with 10 cups water in large, heavy soup pot. Bring to boil, reduce heat and simmer for 3 hours or until beans are tender.

■ Add more water or chicken broth if needed. Make sure there is enough water in pot to make soup consistency and not too thick.

■ Place few cups at a time in food processor (using steel blade) or blender and puree until smooth. Add sour cream and reheat soup. Serve in individual bowls. Serves 8.

Ham Bone, Ham Bone

1 ham hock
1 (10 ounce) package frozen butter beans or lima beans
1½ pounds cooked, cubed ham or chicken
1 (15 ounce) can stewed tomatoes
3 cups small, whole okra
2 large onions, diced
Rice, cooked

■ Boil ham hock in 1½ quarts water in soup pot for about 1 hour 30 minutes.

■ Add remaining ingredients with a little salt and pepper and simmer for additional 1 hour. Remove ham hock and serve over rice. Serves 6.

TIP: Add 1 (15 ounce) can whole potatoes, if desired.

"Hambone, Hambone
Trying to eat
Ketchup on his elbow, pickle on
        his feet
Bread in the basket
Chicken in the stew
Supper on the fire for me and you."
– Hambone (Red Saunders/Leon Washington) Bill Haley

Bonzo Garbanzo Soup

**1 (16 ounce) package frozen chopped bell peppers
and onions
Olive oil
1 pound Italian sausage, cut up
1 (14 ounce) can beef broth
1 (15 ounce) can Italian stewed tomatoes
2 (15 ounce) cans garbanzo beans, rinsed, drained**

- Saute bell peppers and onions in soup pot with a little oil.
  Add Italian sausage and cook until brown. Stir in beef
  broth, stewed tomatoes and garbanzo beans.

- Bring mixture to boil, reduce heat and simmer for about
  30 minutes. Serves 6.

One quart of soup served as a side
dish will be enough for one serving
for six people. For a main course, one
quart will serve three people with two
servings each.

Southwest Pork Stew

2 tablespoons olive oil
2 onions, chopped
1 green bell pepper, seeded, chopped
1 tablespoon minced garlic
2 pounds pork tenderloin, cubed
2 (14 ounce) cans chicken broth
2 baking potatoes, peeled, cubed
2 (15 ounce) cans Mexican stewed tomatoes
2 teaspoons chili powder
1 teaspoon ground cumin
1 tablespoon lime juice

- Place oil in stew pot and saute onion, bell pepper and garlic for 5 minutes.

- Add cubed pork and chicken broth and bring to boil Reduce heat and simmer for 25 minutes.

- Add potatoes and cook for additional 15 minutes or until potatoes are tender.

- Stir in tomatoes, chili powder, cumin, lime juice and a little salt. Heat just until stew is thoroughly hot. Serves 6.

Split Pea and Tortellini Medley

⅓ cup dry split peas
2 tablespoons dried minced onion
1½ teaspoons dried basil
1 tablespoon minced garlic
¾ cup cheese-filled tortellini
1 cup cooked, diced ham
2 (14 ounce) cans chicken broth

- Combine all ingredients with 1½ cups water in soup pot.

- Bring to a boil, reduce heat and simmer for 45 minutes or until peas are tender. Serves 6.

Fresh herbs provide the best flavors. Dried herbs are convenient, affordable and the flavor is more concentrated than fresh herbs. You need to use more than twice the quantity of fresh herbs compared to dried herbs.

Cabbage-Ham Starter

1 (16 ounce) package cabbage slaw
1 onion, chopped
1 teaspoon minced garlic
2 (14 ounce) cans chicken broth
1 (15 ounce) can stewed tomatoes
2 cups cooked, cubed ham
¼ cup packed brown sugar
2 tablespoons lemon juice

- Combine cabbage, onion, garlic, chicken broth and 1 cup water in large, heavy soup pot. Bring to boil, reduce heat and simmer for 20 minutes.

- Stir in tomatoes, ham, 1 teaspoon salt, brown sugar, lemon juice and a little pepper. Heat just until soup is thoroughly hot. Serves 6.

The ladies of the French court of Louis XI mostly ate soups and broth because they believed that chewing would cause wrinkles and ruin their facial features.

No-Brainer Heidelberg Warm-Up

2 (10 ounce) cans potato soup
1 (10 ounce) can cream of celery soup
1 soup can milk
6 slices salami, chopped
10 green onions, chopped

- Cook potato soup, celery soup and milk in large saucepan on medium heat, stirring constantly, just until thoroughly hot.

- Saute salami and onions in sprayed skillet and add to soup.

- Heat thoroughly and serve hot. Serves 6.

You can make a base for any soup by starting with canned soups, broths, prepared soup bases, clam juice, tomato juice and some bacon. Bacon is the secret ingredient that really adds something to canned soups.

Wild Rice-Ham Soup

1 (6 ounce) box long grain-wild rice
1 (16 ounce) package frozen chopped bell peppers
    and onions
1 (10 ounce) can cream of celery soup
2 (14 ounce) cans chicken broth
2 cups cooked, diced ham
2 (15 ounce) cans black-eyed peas and jalapenos
    with liquid

■ Cook rice according to package directions. Combine rice, bell peppers and onions, celery soup, broth, ham, and black-eyed peas in soup pot.

■ Bring to a boil, reduce heat and simmer for 20 minutes. Serves 6.

Savory soups and stews often taste better if made a day or two in advance and reheated just before serving.

Potato-Sausage Feast

1 pound pork sausage links
1 cup chopped celery
1 cup chopped onion
2 (10 ounce) cans potato soup
1 (14 ounce) can chicken broth

- Cut sausage into 1-inch diagonal slices. Brown in large heavy soup pot, drain and place in separate bowl.

- Leave about 2 tablespoons sausage drippings in skillet and saute celery and onion.

- Add potato soup, ¾ cup water, chicken broth and sausage. Bring to boil, reduce heat and simmer for 20 minutes. Serves 4.

TIP: Add 1 cup sliced carrots for more color.

To thicken a broth for a quick-and-easy soup, puree frozen vegetables and add to broth. This will be your base for other ingredients.

Pecos Pork Pot

2 pounds boneless pork shoulder, cubed
Olive oil
1 (16 ounce) package frozen chopped bell peppers
    and onions
2 cloves garlic, minced
½ cup fresh chopped cilantro
3 tablespoons chili powder
2 (14 ounce) cans chicken broth
2 cups peeled, cubed potatoes
1 (16 ounce) package frozen whole kernel corn
Cornbread

- Brown meat in a little oil in large roasting pan. Stir in
  bell peppers and onions, garlic, cilantro, chili powder,
  1 teaspoon salt, and chicken broth.

- Cover and cook on medium heat for about 45 minutes or
  until pork is tender.

- Add potatoes and corn. Bring to a boil, turn heat down to
  medium and cook for additional 30 minutes. Serve with
  cornbread. Serves 6.

Apache Pork and Hominy Soup

2 pounds pork shoulder, cubed
1 onion, chopped
2 ribs celery, sliced
2 (15 ounce) cans yellow hominy with liquid
2 (15 ounce) cans stewed tomatoes
2 (14 ounce) cans chicken broth
1 tablespoon ground cumin
Tortillas
Shredded cheese
Green onions, chopped

- Sprinkle pork cubes with a little salt and pepper and brown in skillet. Place in sprayed 5 to 6-quart slow cooker.

- Combine onion, celery, hominy, stewed tomatoes, broth, cumin and 1 cup water and pour over pork. Cover and cook on HIGH for 6 to 7 hours.

- Serve with warmed, buttered tortillas and top each bowl of soup with some shredded cheese and green onions. Serves 6.

Lucky Black-Eyed Pea Soup

1 onion, chopped
2 cups cooked, cubed ham
2 (15 ounce) cans black-eyed peas with jalapenos
    with liquid
2 ribs celery, sliced
1 (14 ounce) can chicken broth
1 teaspoon minced garlic
1 teaspoon dried sage

■ Combine all ingredients in sprayed slow cooker. Cover and
   cook on LOW for 5 to 7 hours. Serves 4.

*Did you know ice cubes love fat?
Eliminate fat from soup by dropping
ice cubes into your soup pot. As
you stir, the fat will cling to the cubes.*

Chile-Bean Soup

2 (14 ounce) cans chicken broth
3 (15 ounce) cans kidney or black beans, rinsed, drained
2 (10 ounce) cans diced tomatoes and green chilies
1 onion, chopped
1 teaspoon ground cumin
1 tablespoon minced garlic
2 - 3 cups cooked, finely diced ham

- Combine chicken broth and beans in sprayed slow cooker and cook on HIGH just long enough for ingredients to get hot. With potato masher, mash about half of beans in cooker.

- Reduce heat to LOW and add tomatoes and green chilies, onion, cumin, garlic, ham, and ¾ cup water.

- Cover and cook for 5 to 6 hours. Serves 6.

Slow cookers generally retain moisture in a dish rather than cook it off. Condensation and steam build up while cooking. If you want to convert a recipe to cook in the slow cooker, you may want to reduce the amount of liquid in the dish.

Sailor's Slow-Cook Navy Beans

Better than Grandma's!

1½ cups dried navy beans
1 bell pepper, seeded, chopped
1 carrot, finely chopped
2 celery ribs, finely chopped
1 small onion, finely chopped
1 (1 pound) ham hock or 1 cup chopped ham

■ Soak beans for 8 to 12 hours and drain. Place all ingredients in sprayed 2-quart slow cooker, add 5 cups water, ½ teaspoon salt and a little pepper. Cook for 8 to 10 hours on LOW.

■ Remove ham hock and discard skin, fat and bone. Cut meat in small pieces and place in soup. Beans can be mashed, if desired. Serves 4 to 6.

Add a pinch of red pepper flakes to your favorite soup for a flavorful addition.

Bountiful Bean Bake

2 (15 ounce) cans navy beans, rinsed, drained
1 (15 ounce) can butter beans, rinsed, drained
1 (12 ounce) package grated carrots
1 (10 ounce) package frozen chopped bell peppers and
    onions, thawed
2 ribs celery, sliced
1 teaspoon dried marjoram
½ - 1 pound cooked smoked sausage, cut into
    ½-inch slices
½ cup chicken broth

■ Combine beans, carrots, bell peppers and onions, celery, marjoram, sausage, broth and ½ teaspoon salt in sprayed slow cooker.

■ Cover and cook on LOW for 6 to 8 hours. Stir before serving. Serves 6.

TIP: Serve with cornbread and a salad to make a meal.

Whole and fresh spices, herbs and seasonings hold up well and intensify during long cooking times. Ground and dried herbs and spices tend to lose flavor and are best added at the end of cooking.

Stuffed Pork Chops

4 - 5 (1-inch thick) pork chops
1 (15 ounce) can mixed vegetables, well drained
1 (8 ounce) can whole kernel corn, drained
½ cup rice
1 cup Italian-seasoned breadcrumbs
1 (15 ounce) can stewed tomatoes, slightly drained

- Cut pocket in each pork chop and season with a little salt and pepper. Combine vegetables, corn, rice and breadcrumbs in large bowl and stuff pork chops with mixture. Secure open sides with toothpicks.

- Place remaining vegetable mixture in sprayed slow cooker. Add pork chops and spoon stewed tomatoes over top of pork chops. Cover and cook on LOW for 8 to 9 hours. Serves 4 to 5.

In the United States, more tomatoes are consumed than any other single fruit or vegetable!

Our Best Pork Roast

1 (16 ounce) can whole cranberry sauce
½ cup quartered dried apricots
½ teaspoon grated orange peel
⅓ cup orange juice
1 large shallot, chopped
1 tablespoon cider vinegar
1 teaspoon mustard
2 tablespoons brown sugar
¼ teaspoon dried ginger
2 - 3 pound pork loin roast

■ Combine cranberry sauce, apricots, orange peel, orange juice, shallot, vinegar, mustard, brown sugar, ginger and 1 teaspoon salt in bowl. Stir mixture until well blended and spoon into sprayed slow cooker.

■ Trim roast of any fat and add roast to slow cooker. Spoon a little cranberry mixture on top. Cover and cook on LOW for 7 to 9 hours or until pork is tender.

■ Skim off any fat from top of cranberry mixture; place roast on cutting board. Slice pork and top with sauce. Serves 6 to 8.

Italian Pork Chops

6 - 8 (1-inch thick) boneless pork chops
½ pound fresh mushrooms, sliced
1 (10 ounce) package frozen chopped bell peppers and
**   onions, thawed**
1 teaspoon Italian seasoning
1 (15 ounce) can Italian stewed tomatoes

■ Brown pork chops in skillet and sprinkle with salt and
  pepper on both sides.

■ Combine mushrooms, bell peppers and onions, and Italian
  seasoning in sprayed large slow cooker. Place pork chops
  over vegetables and pour stewed tomatoes over pork chops.

■ Cover and cook on LOW for 7 to 8 hours. Serves 6 to 8.

Flavor is often enhanced by browning
meats before adding them to the
slow cooker. Meats can be dredged in
seasoned salt and flour or browned as
is in a little oil. The browning seals in
the flavors and reduces the fat to some
extent. After browning, deglaze the pan
with a little liquid, stir all the bits and
pieces together and cook a little. Add to
slow cooker for more flavor.

Pork Loin Topped with Pecans

½ cup finely ground pecans
1 teaspoon mustard
1 tablespoon brown sugar
1 (3 pound) pork loin
1 (14 ounce) can beef broth
2 tablespoons chili sauce
2 tablespoon lemon juice
1 (10 ounce) box plain couscous

■ Place ground pecans, mustard and brown sugar in small
  bowl and mix well. Press pecan mixture onto pork roast
  and place in sprayed slow cooker.

■ Combine broth, chili sauce and lemon juice in bowl and
  pour into slow cooker. Cover and cook on LOW for
  8 to 10 hours.

■ Let stand for 10 minutes before slicing to serve.

■ Cook couscous according to package directions and place in
  serving bowl. Serve with sliced pork roast. Serves 8 to 10.

Garlic-Roasted Pork Loin

1 (3 - 4 pound) pork loin
4 teaspoons minced garlic
1 tablespoon ketchup
2 tablespoons soy sauce, divided
2 tablespoons plus ½ cup honey, divided
2 tablespoons rice vinegar

- Place pork loin on a sheet of foil. Combine garlic, ketchup, 1 tablespoon soy sauce and 2 tablespoons honey and rub evenly over pork. Place pork loin in sprayed slow cooker. Cover and cook on LOW for 7 to 9 hours.

- Combine remaining soy sauce, remaining ½ cup honey and vinegar in saucepan and cook until hot, about 10 minutes. Slice pork diagonally and place on serving platter. Drizzle sauce over pork slices. Serves 8.

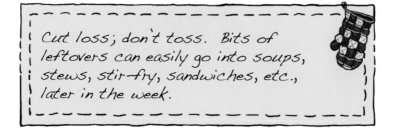

Cut loss; don't toss. Bits of leftovers can easily go into soups, stews, stir-fry, sandwiches, etc., later in the week.

Fruit-Stuffed Pork Roast

1 (3 - 3½ pound) boneless pork loin roast
1 cup mixed dried fruit
1 tablespoon dried onion flakes
1 teaspoon thyme
½ teaspoon ground cinnamon
2 tablespoons canola oil
½ cup apple cider

■ Cut horizontally through center of pork almost to opposite side. Open pork like a book.

■ Layer dried fruit and onion flakes in opening. Bring halves of pork together and tie at 1-inch intervals with kitchen twine.

■ Combine ½ teaspoon salt, thyme, cinnamon and ½ teaspoon pepper in small bowl and rub into roast. Place roast in skillet with oil and brown roast on all sides. Place in sprayed slow cooker and pour apple cider in cooker.

■ Cover and cook on LOW for 3 to 4 hours. Let stand for 10 or 15 minutes before slicing. Serves 6 to 8.

Brown Sugar Glazed Ham

**1 (1 pound) cooked smoked ½-inch thick center
cut ham slice**
⅓ cup orange juice
⅓ cup packed brown sugar
2 teaspoons dijon-style mustard

■ Place ham slice in sprayed slow cooker. Combine juice,
brown sugar and mustard in small bowl. Spread over
ham slice.

■ Cover and cook on LOW for 3 to 4 hours or until ham
has glossy glaze. Cut ham into individual servings.
Serves 4 to 5.

If you have any leftover cooked
pasta, meat or vegetables, use them
for soup ingredients. Most cooked
vegetables can also be pureed and stirred
in to thicken soups.

Cherry Ham Loaf

Great for leftover ham

1½ pounds cooked, ground ham
1 pound ground turkey
2 eggs
1 cup seasoned breadcrumbs
2 teaspoons chicken seasoning

- Make foil handles for meat loaf (see page 233).

- Combine all ingredients in bowl and mix well. Shape into
  short loaf that fits into sprayed oval slow cooker. Cover and
  cook on LOW for 4 to 5 hours. Serve with Cherry Sauce.

Cherry Sauce:

1 cup cherry preserves
2 tablespoons cider vinegar
Scant ⅛ teaspoon ground cloves
Scant ⅛ teaspoon ground cinnamon

- Place cherry preserves, vinegar, cloves and cinnamon
  in saucepan and heat. Serve over slices of ham loaf.
  Serves 4 to 6.

Florentine-Style Soup

3 - 4 large potatoes, peeled, diced
1 onion, finely diced
1 (1 pound) ham hock
1 (32 ounce) carton chicken broth
1½ teaspoons seasoned salt
½ teaspoon dry mustard
1 (10 ounce) package frozen chopped spinach, thawed,
**   well drained***
1 cup shredded cheddar or Swiss cheese

■ Combine potatoes, onion, ham hock (or 2 cups diced ham), broth, seasoned salt, a little pepper and mustard in sprayed slow cooker. Cover and cook on LOW for 7 to 8 hours.

■ Remove ham hock, chop meat and discard bone; return meat to slow cooker. Increase heat to HIGH; add spinach; cover and cook for additional 20 minutes. Add cheese and stir until it melts. Serves 4 to 6.

TIP: Squeeze spinach between paper towels to remove excess moisture.

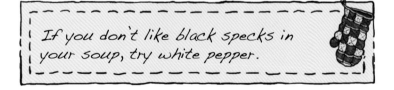

If you don't like black specks in your soup, try white pepper.

Ben's Ham and Rice

1 (6.7 ounce) box brown-wild rice, mushroom recipe
3 - 4 cups cooked, chopped or cubed ham
1 (4 ounce) can sliced mushrooms, drained
1 (10 ounce) package frozen green peas
2 cups chopped celery

- Combine rice, seasoning packet, ham, mushrooms, peas, and celery plus 2⅔ cups water in sprayed slow cooker. Stir to mix well.

- Cover and cook on LOW for 2 to 4 hours. Serves 4 to 6.

Delectable Apricot Ribs

4 - 5 pounds baby back pork ribs
1 (16 ounce) jar apricot preserves
⅓ cup soy sauce
¼ cup packed light brown sugar
2 teaspoons garlic powder
¼ cup apple cider vinegar

- Place ribs in sprayed slow cooker.

- Combine preserves, soy sauce, brown sugar, garlic powder and vinegar in bowl and spoon over ribs.

- Cover and cook on LOW for 6 to 7 hours. Serves 8 to 10.

Barbecued Ribs

4 - 5 pounds pork spareribs, cut into 2-rib pieces
1 cup spicy ketchup
¼ cup vinegar
⅔ cup packed brown sugar
1 tablespoon Worcestershire sauce

■ Preheat broiler.

■ Place spareribs on rack in shallow baking pan and brown for
10 to 15 minutes on each side. Drain and place in sprayed
slow cooker.

■ Combine ketchup, vinegar, brown sugar, Worcestershire
and ½ teaspoon salt in small bowl. Pour mixture over ribs;
turning ribs to evenly coat.

■ Cover and cook on LOW for 5 to 6 hours or until ribs are
tender. Serves 6.

The March 2000 edition of the
American Medical Association's
Archives of Family Medicine stated that
eating meals at home during the week is
directly associated with better nutrition
in children. They got more nutrients
such as calcium, iron, fiber, vitamin B6,
vitamin C, and vitamin E and consumed less
fat eating at home than eating out.

Perfect Pork Chops and Potatoes

2 tablespoons canola oil
6 - 8 boneless pork chops
1 (10 ounce) can cream of chicken soup
1 tablespoon mustard
½ cup chicken broth
1 teaspoon minced garlic
6 - 8 red potatoes with peels, sliced
2 - 3 onions, sliced

■ Heat oil in skillet on medium-high heat and brown pork chops on both sides.

■ Combine soup, mustard, broth, garlic and a little salt and pepper in sprayed slow cooker. Layer potatoes and onions over mixture; place browned pork chops on top.

■ Cover and cook on LOW for 8 to 10 hours or on HIGH for 4 to 5 hours. Serves 6 to 8.

Large or firm vegetables like potatoes, onions and carrots cook more slowly than meat. Put these vegetables in the slow cooker first and put the meat on top of them.

Mama Mia Meat Loaf

1 (15 ounce) jar spaghetti sauce, divided
1 pound Italian pork sausage, removed from casing
1 pound ground beef
1 cup breadcrumbs
1 cup chopped onion
1 cup grated parmesan cheese
1 teaspoon minced garlic
1 egg

■ Make foil handles for meat loaf (see page 233).

■ Combine ½ cup spaghetti sauce, 1 teaspoon each of salt
and pepper, and all remaining ingredients in large bowl; mix
well. Form into loaf in sprayed slow cooker.

■ Pour remaining sauce over loaf. Cover and cook on LOW
for 5 to 7 hours. Serves 8.

Have old memories,
but keep young hopes.

Spiked Crab Pot

1 (1 ounce) packet onion soup mix
1 (6 ounce) can crabmeat with liquid, flaked
1 (8 ounce) carton whipping cream
½ cup white wine

■ Dissolve soup mix with 2 cups water in saucepan.

■ Add crabmeat, crab liquid and whipping cream. Season
with a little salt and pepper.

■ Heat, but do not boil, and simmer for 20 minutes.

■ Stir in wine, heat and serve warm. Serves 4.

Wine is a great flavor addition to
soups and stews. When using wine
or alcohol in soup, use less salt
because the wine tends to intensify
saltiness. About ¼ cup wine should be
used for each quart of soup.

Fresh Oyster Boat

2 (14 ounce) cans chicken broth
1 large onion, chopped
3 ribs celery, sliced
2 teaspoons minced garlic
2 (1 pint) cartons fresh oysters, rinsed, drained
½ cup (1 stick) butter
¼ cup flour
2 cups milk
1 tablespoon dried parsley

- Combine broth, onion, celery and garlic in soup pot. Bring to boil, reduce heat and simmer, stirring occasionally for 30 minutes.

- Boil oysters in 2 cups water in saucepan for 2 minutes, stirring often or until edges of oysters begin to curl.

- Remove oysters with slotted spoon, coarsely chop half and set aside. Pour oyster stock into soup pot with vegetables.

- Melt butter in saucepan over medium heat, gradually whisk in flour and cook for 1 minute. Add flour mixture to soup pot and simmer, stirring occasionally over medium heat for 3 minutes.

- Stir in chopped oysters, milk, parsley and a little salt and pepper. Cook and stir occasionally over medium heat for 8 minutes or until mixture thickens. Stir in remaining whole oysters. Serves 6 to 8.

Homestyle Seafood Chowder

¼ cup (½ stick) butter
1 (8 ounce) package frozen salad shrimp, thawed
1 (6 ounce) can crab, drained, flaked
1 (15 ounce) can whole new potatoes,
    drained, chopped
1 teaspoon minced garlic
½ cup flour
2 (14 ounce) cans chicken broth, divided
1 cup half-and-half cream

- Melt butter in large saucepan on medium heat. Add shrimp, crab, new potatoes and garlic and cook for 10 minutes.

- Stir in flour and cook, stirring constantly for 3 minutes. Gradually add chicken broth, cook and stir until mixture thickens.

- Stir in half-and-half cream and a little salt and pepper, stirring constantly and cook just until mixture is thoroughly hot; do not boil. Serves 6.

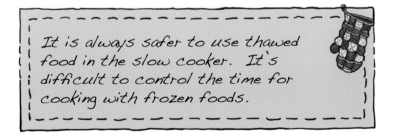

It is always safer to use thawed food in the slow cooker. It's difficult to control the time for cooking with frozen foods.

Cauliflower-Crab Chowder

1 (16 ounce) package frozen cauliflower
¼ cup (½ stick) butter
¼ cup flour
1 (14 ounce) can chicken broth
1½ cups milk
1 (3 ounce) package cream cheese, cubed
1 (2 ounce) jar chopped pimento, drained
1 (8 ounce) package refrigerated, imitation crabmeat,
   drained

■ Cook cauliflower in ¾ cup water in large saucepan until
  tender-crisp.

■ In separate saucepan, melt butter, stir in flour and mix
  well. Add broth, milk and cream cheese and cook, stirring
  constantly, until thick and bubbly.

■ Add mixture to saucepan with cauliflower and stir in
  pimento and a little salt and pepper.

■ Stir in crab and heat just until thoroughly hot. Serves 4.

Harbor Cod-Corn Chowder

8 slices bacon
1 pound cod, cut into bite-size pieces
2 large baking potatoes, thinly sliced
3 ribs celery, sliced
1 onion, chopped
1 (15 ounce) can whole kernel corn
1 (8 ounce) carton whipping cream

■ Fry bacon in large, heavy soup pot, remove bacon and drain. Crumble bacon and set aside.

■ Drain fat from soup pot and stir in 2½ cups water, cod, potatoes, celery, onion, corn and a little salt and pepper. Bring to boil, reduce heat, cover and simmer for about 20 minutes or until fish and potatoes are done.

■ Stir in cream and heat just until chowder is thoroughly hot. When serving, sprinkle crumbled bacon over each serving. Serves 6.

TIP: Other seafood such as lobster, clams and other varieties of fish work well in this dish

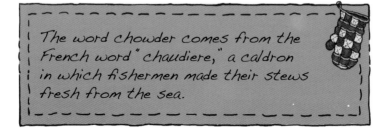

The word chowder comes from the French word "chaudiere," a caldron in which fishermen made their stews fresh from the sea.

'Who Dat' Seafood Gumbo

¼ cup (½ stick) butter
¼ cup flour
1½ - 2 pounds fresh okra, sliced
2 (15 ounce) cans whole tomatoes, chopped
½ cup minced onion
1 pound shrimp, peeled, cleaned
1 pound crabmeat, flaked, drained
1 (1 pint) carton fresh oysters with liquor
Rice, cooked

■ Melt butter in heavy skillet and add flour. Stir well over medium heat to make smooth, paste-like roux.

■ When roux is rich brown color, add a little salt and pepper and mix well. Add 2 quarts water, okra, tomatoes and onion. Cook on low for 20 minutes.

■ Add all seafood and cook on medium-low for 30 minutes or until desired consistency. Serve over rice. Serves 8.

TIP: Garnish with sliced green onions, shrimp or crawfish.

If you don't want all seafood, add smoked sausage.

Succulent Crab Chowder

3 medium red potatoes, cut into ½-inch cubes
1 (16 ounce) package frozen corn, thawed
2 ribs celery, sliced
½ cup finely chopped red bell pepper
1 teaspoon dried thyme
1 (32 ounce) carton chicken broth
1 (8 ounce) carton whipping cream
⅓ cup cornstarch
2 (6 ounce) cans crabmeat, drained

- Layer potatoes, corn, celery and bell pepper in sprayed slow cooker. Sprinkle with thyme and a little pepper. Stir in chicken broth, cover and cook on LOW for 4 hours.

- Combine cream and cornstarch in bowl and slowly stir into slow cooker. Increase heat to HIGH, cover and cook for 1 additional hour. Stir in crabmeat and serve hot. Serves 4 to 6.

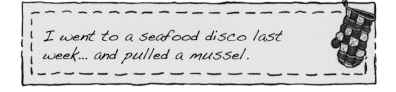

I went to a seafood disco last week... and pulled a mussel.

Easy Oyster Stew

4 green onions, finely chopped
½ cup (1 stick) butter, melted
1 teaspoon Worcestershire sauce
2 (12 ounce) containers fresh oysters with liquid
1 (8 ounce) carton whipping cream
3 cups milk
Dash of cayenne pepper

- Combine onions, butter and Worcestershire in sprayed slow cooker. Cover and cook on LOW for 2 hours or until mixture is hot.

- Stir in oysters with liquid, cream, milk, cayenne pepper and a little salt. Cover and cook for about 30 minutes or until oyster edges begin to curl and stew is thoroughly hot. Serves 6.

*It was a brave man
who first ate an oyster.*

Cheesy Veggie-Crab Casserole

3 tablespoons plus ¼ cup (½ stick) butter, divided
2 ribs celery, thinly sliced
1 (10 ounce) package frozen chopped bell peppers and
    onions, thawed
¼ cup flour
2 (14 ounce) cans chicken broth
1¼ cups instant rice
2 (6 once) cans crabmeat, drained, flaked
1 cup shredded cheddar cheese
1 (4 ounce) can sliced mushrooms, drained
½ cup sliced almonds
1 cup seasoned breadcrumbs

■ Melt 3 tablespoons butter in skillet on medium heat and
  lightly saute celery and bell peppers and onions. Add flour
  and stir well. Slowly add chicken broth, stirring constantly
  and cook until slightly thickened.

■ Combine rice, crabmeat, cheese, mushrooms and almonds
  in bowl. Stir in sauce and transfer to sprayed slow cooker.
  Cover and cook on HIGH for 3 to 5 hours.

■ Spoon contents of slow cooker into ovenproof serving dish.
  Melt ¼ cup (½ stick) butter and combine with breadcrumbs
  in small bowl; sprinkle over contents of serving dish. Place
  under broiler until crumbs are slightly brown. Serves 5 to 6.

Yummy Tuna Bake

2 (6 ounce) cans white tuna, drained, flaked
1 (10 ounce) can cream of chicken soup
3 eggs, hard-boiled, chopped
3 ribs celery, thinly sliced
1 red bell pepper, seeded, chopped
½ cup coarsely chopped pecans
½ cup mayonnaise
2 cups crushed potato chips, divided

- Combine tuna, soup, eggs, celery, bell pepper, pecans, mayonnaise, 1 teaspoon pepper, half potato chips and a little salt in bowl and mix well.

- Transfer to sprayed slow cooker. Cover and cook on LOW for 5 to 7 hours. When ready to serve, sprinkle remaining potato chips on top. Serves 4 to 5.

Because the lid forms a seal with the slow cooker, there is very little evaporation of the cooking liquid.
If a stovetop recipe is converted to the slow cooker method, the amount of liquid used (water, broth, etc.) should be reduced. Liquid can be added later if needed.

Super Shrimp and Rice

1 (16 ounce) package frozen shrimp, thawed
¾ cup chicken broth
1 red bell pepper, seeded, cut into strips
1 (10 ounce) package frozen okra, thawed
1 teaspoon chili powder
¼ teaspoon dried oregano
¼ cup (½ stick) butter, melted
¼ cup sun-dried tomatoes, sliced
2 cups cooked rice

- Combine shrimp, broth, bell pepper, okra, chili powder, oregano and butter in sprayed slow cooker. Cover and cook on LOW for 2 hours.

- Stir in tomatoes and rice; cover and cook for additional 15 minutes or until mixture is thoroughly hot. Serves 4 to 6.

Wrinkles don't hurt.

Poached Halibut or Salmon

¼ cup (½ stick)
2 tablespoons flour
1 tablespoon sugar
⅓ cup dry white wine
⅔ cup milk
2 pounds halibut or salmon steaks

- Melt butter in medium saucepan over low heat. Add flour and sugar and stir to dissolve. Add wine and milk and bring to a boil; reduce heat. Add ½ teaspoon salt.

- Stir constantly until sauce thickens, about 5 minutes. Place fish in sprayed slow cooker and pour sauce over top.

- Cook on HIGH for about 2 hours 30 minutes to 3 hours. Serves 4.

Desserts,
Slow Cooker

Good-Time Apple Crisp

½ cup flour
1½ cups sugar, divided
½ teaspoon ground cinnamon, divided
¼ cup (½ stick) butter, cut in pieces
½ cup chopped pecans
2 teaspoons lemon juice
¼ teaspoon ground ginger
5 - 6 Granny Smith apples, peeled, cut into wedges
Vanilla ice cream

■ Combine flour, ½ cup sugar, ¼ teaspoon cinnamon and butter pieces in bowl. Work butter into flour mixture with pastry blender or fork until mixture becomes coarse crumbs. Stir in pecans.

■ In separate bowl, whisk remaining sugar, remaining cinnamon, lemon juice and ginger. Add apple wedges and toss for mixture to cover apples. Transfer to sprayed slow cooker and sprinkle flour-pecan mixture over apples.

■ Cover and cook on LOW for 4 hours or on HIGH for 2 hours. Serve warm or at room temperature with a dip of vanilla ice cream. Serves 6 to 8.

Chocolate Party Fondue

Your slow cooker can easily become a fondue pot.

2 (7 ounce) bars chocolate, chopped
1 (4 ounce) bar white chocolate, chopped
1 (7 ounce) jar marshmallow creme
¾ cup half-and-half cream
½ cup slivered almonds, chopped, toasted
¼ cup amaretto liqueur
Pound cake and fruit

■ Combine chocolate bars, white chocolate bar, marshmallow creme, half-and-half cream and almonds in small, sprayed slow cooker.

■ Cover and cook on LOW for about 2 hours or until chocolates melt.

■ Stir to mix well and fold in amaretto liqueur. Cut pound cake into small squares and dip into fondue. Fruits such as strawberries, grapes, slices of apple, pear, kiwi and bananas, just to name a few are great too. Serves 8 to 10.

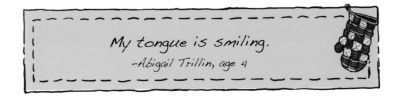

My tongue is smiling.
—Abigail Trillin, age 4

Blueberry Goodness

1 (20 ounce) can blueberry pie filling
1 (18 ounce) box yellow cake mix
½ cup (1 stick) butter, softened
1 cup chopped walnuts
Vanilla ice cream

■ Place pie filling in sprayed slow cooker. Combine cake mix, butter and walnuts and spread over pie filling.

■ Cover and cook on LOW for 2 hours. Serve over ice cream. Serves 8 to 10.

Once food has been cooked and served, it is best to remove the food from the ceramic insert to refrigerate. The liners of slow cookers are made of very heavy material and do not cool quickly. This can enable the growth of harmful bacteria.

Slow Cooker Bananas Foster

5 bananas, sliced
½ cup packed brown sugar
½ cup (1 stick) butter, melted
¼ cup rum, optional
Vanilla ice cream

- Mix brown sugar, butter and rum in sprayed slow cooker. Add banana slices and coat with brown sugar mixture. Cook on LOW for 1 hour.

- Remove bananas from slow cooker and pour over individual bowls of ice cream. Serve immediately. Serves 4.

TIP: If you want Bananas Foster to flame, do not add rum to slow cooker. After you pour bananas over ice cream, pour 151-proof rum over bananas. Light the rum with a match just after you serve it and it will flame briefly for a nice effect.

Bananas Foster was created in 1951 at Brennan's Restaurant in New Orleans. It was named for Richard Foster, the chairman of the New Orleans Crime Commission and a friend of the founder of Brennan's.

Delicious Bread Pudding

8 cups cubed leftover hot rolls, cinnamon rolls or bread
2 cups milk
4 large eggs
¾ cup sugar
⅓ cup packed brown sugar
¼ cup (½ stick) butter, melted
1 teaspoon vanilla
¼ teaspoon ground nutmeg
1 cup finely chopped pecans
Frozen whipped topping, thawed

■ Place cubed bread or rolls in sprayed slow cooker.

■ Combine milk, eggs, sugar, brown sugar, butter, vanilla and nutmeg in bowl and beat until smooth. Stir in pecans and pour over bread.

■ Cover and cook on LOW for 3 hours. Serve with whipped topping. Serves 8.

Honey was the only sweetener in Europe until sugar was imported in the Middle Ages. It was very expensive and considered a luxury for the wealthy. It's only within the past two centuries that the use of sugar became commonplace.

Slow Chocolate Fix

1 (18 ounce) box chocolate cake mix
1 (8 ounce) carton sour cream
4 eggs, beaten
¾ cup canola oil
1 (3.4 ounce) box instant chocolate pudding mix
¾ cup chopped pecans
Vanilla ice cream

■ Mix cake mix, sour cream, eggs, oil, pudding mix, pecans and 1 cup water in bowl. Pour into sprayed slow cooker.

■ Cover and cook on LOW for 6 to 8 hours. Serve warm with vanilla ice cream. Serves 6 to 8.

Maybe the little things, like having a meal at the table, are more important than we realize. Maybe these little things are the things we never forget... our memories and family traditions.

Index

C

Cookbooks Published by Cookbook Resources, LLC
Bringing Family and Friends to the Table

The Best 1001 Short, Easy Recipes
1001 Slow Cooker Recipes
1001 Short, Easy, Inexpensive Recipes
1001 Fast Easy Recipes
1001 America's Favorite Recipes
1001 Easy Inexpensive Grilling Recipes
1,001 Easy Potluck Recipes
1,001 Comfort Food Recipes
Easy Slow Cooker Cookbook
Busy Woman's Slow Cooker Recipes
Busy Woman's Quick & Easy Recipes
Easy Meals-in-Minutes
365 Easy Soups and Stews
365 Easy Chicken Recipes
365 Easy One-Dish Recipes
365 Easy Soup Recipes
365 Easy Vegetarian Recipes
365 Easy Casserole Recipes
365 Easy Pasta Recipes
365 Easy Slow Cooker Recipes
Super Simple Cupcake Recipes
Easy Garden Fresh Recipes & Homemade
Preserves (Photos)
Easy Soups and Slow Cooker Recipes (Photos)
Leaving Home Cookbook and Survival Guide
Essential 3-4-5 Ingredient Recipes
Ultimate 4 Ingredient Cookbook
Easy Cooking with 5 Ingredients
The Best of Cooking with 3 Ingredients
Easy Diabetic Recipes
Ultimate 4 Ingredient Diabetic Cookbook
4-Ingredient Recipes for 30-Minute Meals
Cooking with Beer
The Washington Cookbook
The Pennsylvania Cookbook
The California Cookbook
Best-Loved Canadian Recipes
Best-Loved Recipes from the Pacific Northwest

Easy Homemade Preserves (Photos)
Garden Fresh Recipes (Photos)
Easy Slow Cooker Recipes (Photos)
Cool Smoothies (Photos)
Easy Cupcake Recipes (Photos)
Easy Soup Recipes (Photos)
Classic Tex-Mex and Texas Cooking
Best-Loved Southern Recipes
Classic Southwest Cooking
Miss Sadie's Southern Cooking
Classic Pennsylvania Dutch Cooking
The Quilters' Cookbook
Healthy Cooking with 4 Ingredients
Trophy Hunter's Wild Game Cookbook
Recipe Keeper
Simple Old-Fashioned Baking
Old-Fashioned Cookies
Quick Fixes with Cake Mixes
Kitchen Keepsakes & More Kitchen Keepsakes
Cookbook 25 Years
Texas Longhorn Cookbook
The Authorized Texas Ranger Cookbook
Gifts for the Cookie Jar
All New Gifts for the Cookie Jar
The Big Bake Sale Cookbook
Easy One-Dish Meals
Easy Potluck Recipes
Easy Casseroles Cookbook
Easy Desserts
Sunday Night Suppers
Easy Church Suppers
365 Easy Meals
Gourmet Cooking with 5 Ingredients
Muffins In A Jar
A Little Taste of Texas
A Little Taste of Texas II
Ultimate Gifts for the Cookie Jar

cookbook
resources LLC

www.cookbookresources.com
Toll-Free 866-229-2665
Your Ultimate Source for Easy Cookbooks

What's What:
Soups, Stews, Chowders and Chilis

Soups

Most of us know or have a pretty good idea of the difference between **soups** and **stews**. Soups are thin and stews are thick. It's very simple. But if you want to know more about these comforting dishes, look deeper to learn about many other differences.

Soups start with liquid, usually hot water. Meats, beans and vegetables are simmered to extract the flavors of the ingredients and that is the broth or stock used as the base. As they boil they break down and mix with the liquid for a distinctive blend of flavors.

Clear soups are called broth, bouillon or consommé. Purées are mixes of vegetables and liquid thickened by the starch in the vegetables. Other types of purées are thickened with cream, milk, eggs, rice, flour or grains.

Stews

Stews are very similar to **soups** because they are combinations of vegetables and meats cooked in a broth or stock. They are thickened with most of the same ingredients as **soups**, but there is a distinct difference. **Stews** usually have larger pieces of meat and vegetables than do **soups**. These large pieces are simmered for a long time to tenderize the ingredients.

Stews are usually served as a main course and **soups** are usually served as a first course. **Stews** are usually heartier and more filling than **soups**, but there is little difference in the popularity of both.

continued next page...

Continued from previous page...

Chowders

Chowders are similar to stews, but mainly consist of fish or clams, potatoes, and onions. New England clam **chowder** has a cream base and Manhattan clam **chowder** has a tomato base. There is also corn **chowder** with a cream base.

Gumbos and Jambalayas

Gumbo and **jambalaya** are also soups. **Gumbo** is considered the "king of soups" by people in Louisiana. Both are combinations of meat, vegetables, a rich stock base and rice. Created in southern Louisiana, both have storied traditions and are very popular in the South.

Chilis

Chiles with an "e" refers to the many peppers available for cooking. **Chili** with an "i" refers to the state dish of Texas. Dallas' Frank Tolbert, the founder of the International Terlingua Chili Cook-off and chili aficionado, called **chili** "a bowl of red" to reflect the proper color of the dish. The color and ingredients of **chili** may open a can of beans.

DEDICATION

Cookbook Resources' mission is

Bringing Family and Friends to the Table.

We recognize the importance of shared meals as a means of building family bonds with memories and traditions that will last a lifetime. At mealtimes we share more than food. We share ourselves.

This cookbook is dedicated with gratitude and respect to all those who show their love by making home-cooked meals and bringing family and friends to the table.

Great memories begin with great food.

www.cookbookresources.com
Toll-free 1-866-229-2665
Your Ultimate Source for Easy Cookbooks